Power Maths

Year 2 Practice Book 2B

What did you learn last term in maths?

Draw or write one thing you remember.

This book belongs to _____ .

My class is _____ .

Pearson

Contents

We will practise different ways to solve problems!

It is time to continue our maths journey!

3

How to use this book

Do you remember how to use this Practice Book?

Use the Textbook first to learn how to solve this type of problem.

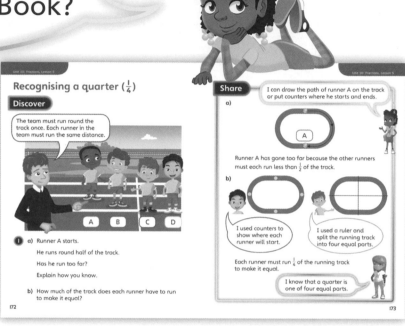

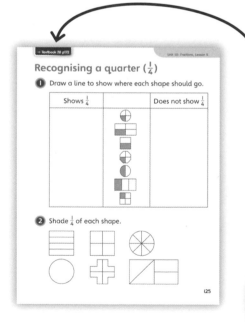

This shows you which Textbook page to use.

Have a go at questions by yourself using this Practice Book. Use what you have learned.

 Challenge questions make you think hard!

 Questions with this light bulb make you think differently.

Reflect

Each lesson ends with a Reflect question so you can show how much you have learned.

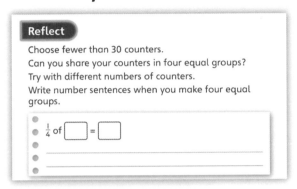

Reflect

Choose fewer than 30 counters.
Can you share your counters in four equal groups?
Try with different numbers of counters.
Write number sentences when you make four equal groups.

$\frac{1}{4}$ of ☐ = ☐

Show what you have done in My Power Points at the back of this book.

My journal

At the end of a unit your teacher will ask you to fill in My journal.

This will help you show how much you can do now that you have finished the unit.

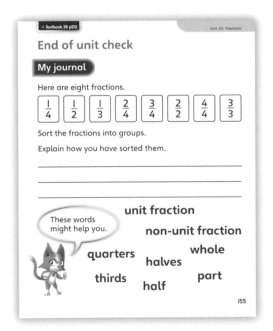

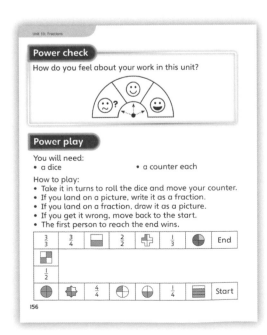

→ Textbook 2B p8

Making equal groups

1 Jo makes towers of 5 blocks each.

She has 20 blocks in total.

How many towers can she make?

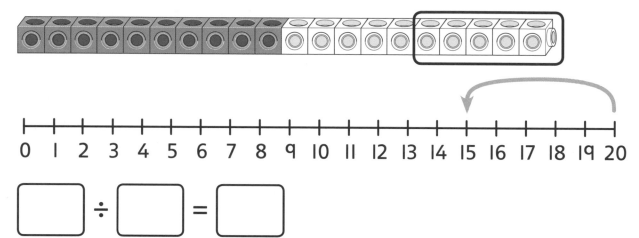

$$\boxed{} \div \boxed{} = \boxed{}$$

Jo can make $\boxed{}$ towers of 5 blocks.

2 Complete each number sentence.

a)

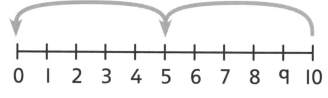

$10 \div 5 = \boxed{}$

b)

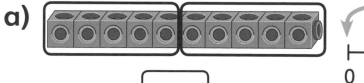

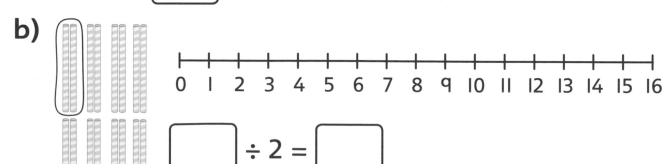

$\boxed{} \div 2 = \boxed{}$

3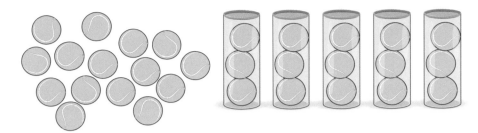

$15 \div 3 = 5$

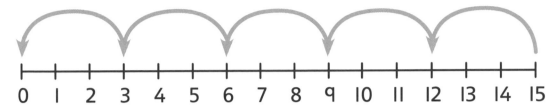

0 1 2 3 4 5 6 7 8 9 10 11 12 13 14 15

Who is correct?

There are 15 tennis balls in total.
They are put in groups of 5.
There are 3 equal groups at the end.

There are 15 tennis balls in total.
They are put in groups of 3.
There are 5 equal groups at the end.

I think _____ is right.

_____ made a mistake about

_____ .

4 Which makes the most groups?

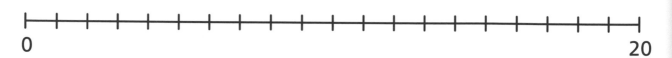

CHALLENGE

$20 \div 5$ $20 \div 10$ $20 \div 2$

0   20

0   20

0   20

☐ ÷ ☐ makes the most groups.

This is because _____ .

Reflect

There are 15 .

5 fit on one tray.

Write a division to show how many trays are needed.

☐ ÷ ☐ = ☐

Show it on a number line.

Sharing and grouping

1 Jamal has 15 flowers.

He shares them equally between 5 vases.

How many flowers go in each vase?

$15 \div 5 = \boxed{}$

There are $\boxed{}$ flowers in each vase.

2 There are 15 bricks.

They are shared between three wheelbarrows.

How many bricks go in each wheelbarrow?

$\boxed{} \div \boxed{} = \boxed{}$

Each wheelbarrow carries $\boxed{}$ bricks.

3 It is sports day. Share the equipment between 4 classes.

a) □ ÷ □ = □

Each class gets □ 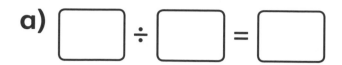 .

b) □ ÷ □ = □

Each class gets □ ● .

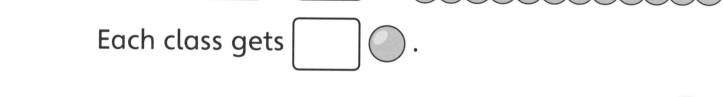

4 Use these words to complete each sentence.

shared	carrots
total	rabbits
people	equal

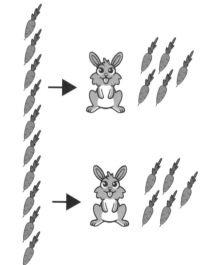

$10 ÷ 2 = 5$

The 10 represents _____.

The 2 represents _____.

The 5 represents _____.

CHALLENGE

5 Draw lines to match the sentences. Then complete a number sentence for each pair.

I shared  between 4 people.

Each person had 10.

I shared ⬜ between 2 people.

Each person had 5.

⬜ ◯ 4 = ⬜

20 ◯ ⬜ = ⬜

Reflect

Draw a picture to show 10  shared between 5 people.

Complete a division to represent this.

⬜ ◯ ⬜ = ⬜

What does each number and sign represent?

→ **Textbook 2B p16**

Dividing by 2

1 How many pairs of swans are in the pond?

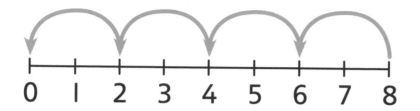

$8 ÷ 2 = \boxed{}$

There are $\boxed{}$ pairs of swans.

2 There are 14 pegs. They are used to hang  .

2 pegs hang each .

How many can be hung up?

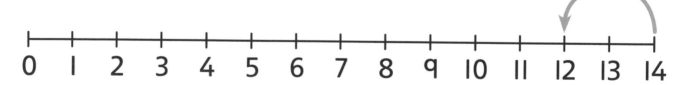

$14 ÷ \boxed{} = \boxed{}$

$\boxed{}$  can be hung up.

12

3 Write a multiplication and a division for each picture.

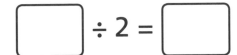

$\boxed{} \times 2 = \boxed{}$

$\boxed{} \div 2 = \boxed{}$

$\boxed{} \times 2 = \boxed{}$

$\boxed{} \div 2 = \boxed{}$

4 Complete each number sentence.

$\boxed{} \times 2 = \boxed{}$

$\boxed{} \div 2 = \boxed{}$

$\boxed{} \times 2 = \boxed{}$

$\boxed{} \div 2 = \boxed{}$

$\boxed{} \times 2 = \boxed{}$

$\boxed{} \div 2 = \boxed{}$

$\boxed{} \times 2 = \boxed{}$

$\boxed{} \div 2 = \boxed{}$

5 Match each division to a times-table fact.

Complete the divisions.

$8 \div 2 = \boxed{}$

$\boxed{} \div 2 = 8$

$2 \div 2 = \boxed{}$

$\boxed{} \div 2 = 2$

$\boxed{} \div 2 = 5$

$\boxed{} \div 2 = 7$

$1 \times 2 = 2$

$2 \times 2 = 4$

$3 \times 2 = 6$

$4 \times 2 = 8$

$5 \times 2 = 10$

$6 \times 2 = 12$

$7 \times 2 = 14$

$8 \times 2 = 16$

Reflect

I know that $5 \times 2 = 10$.

So I know $10 \div 2 = \boxed{}$ because _____

_____

_____

Odd and even numbers

1 The children must work in pairs.

Will anyone be on their own?

There are ☐ children.

There will be ☐ on their own.

So ☐ is an _____ number.

There are ☐ children.

There will be ☐ on their own.

So ☐ is an _____ number.

2 Circle pairs. Write the number and then 'odd' or 'even' to complete the answers below.

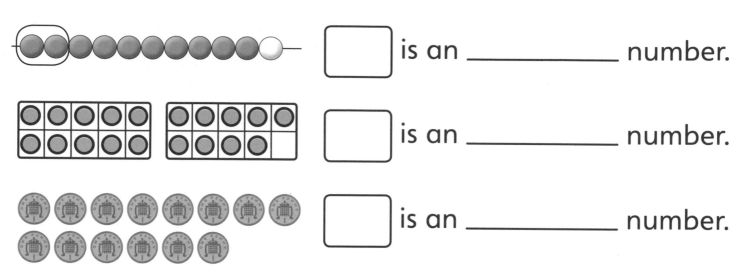

☐ is an _____ number.

☐ is an _____ number.

☐ is an _____ number.

3 Tick which pictures show odd numbers.

Use the 2 times-table to help you decide.

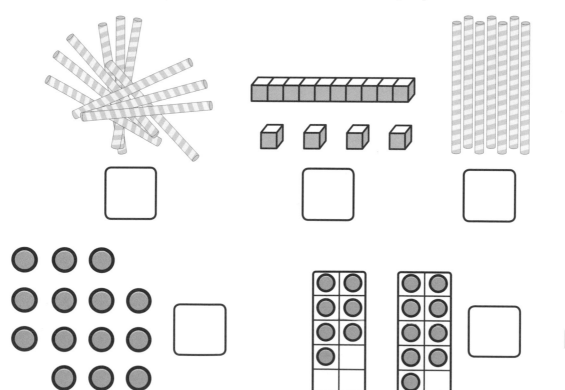

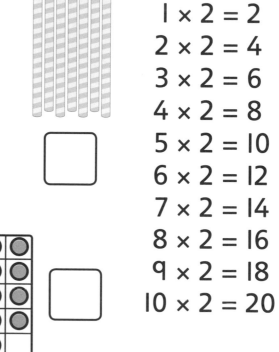

$1 \times 2 = 2$
$2 \times 2 = 4$
$3 \times 2 = 6$
$4 \times 2 = 8$
$5 \times 2 = 10$
$6 \times 2 = 12$
$7 \times 2 = 14$
$8 \times 2 = 16$
$9 \times 2 = 18$
$10 \times 2 = 20$

4

| 4 | 16 | 5 | 9 | 11 | 14 | 6 | 15 |

CHALLENGE

James chose an even number.

Rani chose a number that is 5 away from James's number.

What two cards did they pick? _____

Can you find a different answer? _____

Reflect

Jamal is trying to group 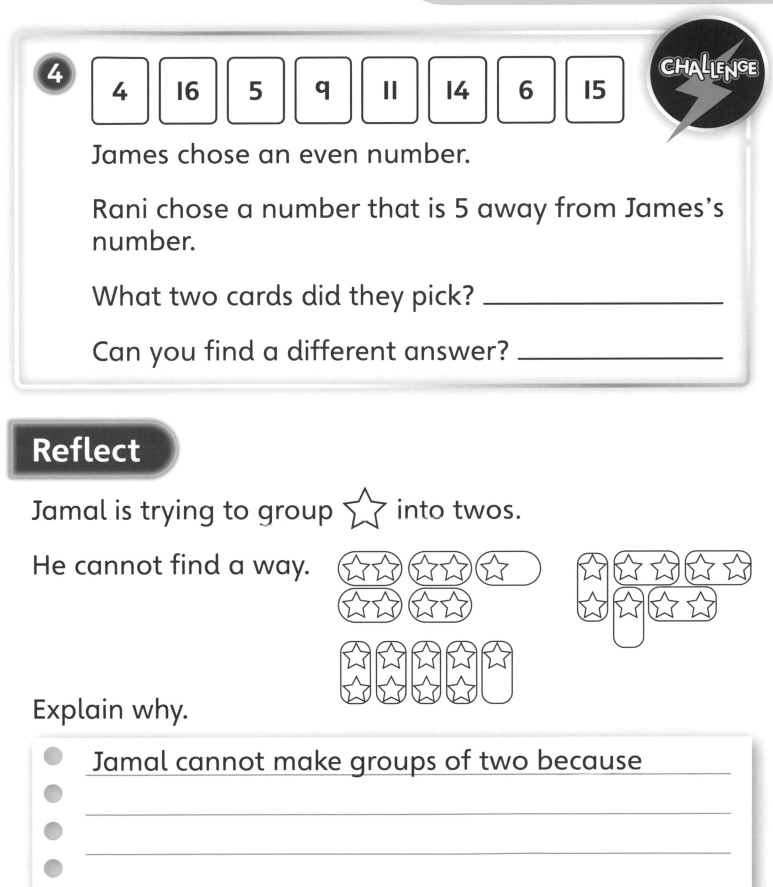 into twos.

He cannot find a way.

Explain why.

Jamal cannot make groups of two because _____

_____

_____

_____

_____

→ Textbook 2B p24

Dividing by 5

1 Jamal has won 15 ☆.

He puts 5 ☆ on each page of his book.

How many pages does he fill?

15 ÷ 5 = ☐

2 Tao has 30 straws.

She makes a house shape using 5 straws.

How many houses can she make?

30 ÷ ☐ = ☐

Tao can make ☐ houses.

18

3 Use the 5 times-table to help you complete the number sentences.

1 × 5 ●●●●●

2 × 5 ●●●●●○○○○○

3 × 5 ●●●●●○○○○○●●●●●

4 × 5 ●●●●●○○○○○●●●●●○○○○○

5 × 5 ●●●●●○○○○○●●●●●○○○○○●●●●●

6 × 5 ●●●●●○○○○○●●●●●○○○○○●●●●●○○○○○

7 × 5 ●●●●●○○○○○●●●●●○○○○○●●●●●○○○○○●●●●●

$2 \times 5 = 10$

$10 \div 5 = \boxed{}$

$\boxed{} \times 5 = 25$

$25 \div 5 = \boxed{}$

$4 \times 5 = 20$

$20 \div 5 = \boxed{}$

$7 \times 5 = \boxed{}$

$\boxed{} \div 5 = 7$

4 Complete each number fact.

$15 \div 5 = 3$

$\boxed{} \div 5 = 4$

$\boxed{} \div 5 = 5$

$45 \div 5 = 9$

$\boxed{} \div 5 = 8$

$\boxed{} \div 5 = 7$

5

| 5 | 10 | 15 | 20 | 25 | 30 | 35 | 40 | 45 |

CHALLENGE

Malik chose one of these numbers.

He divided it by 5. The answer was an even number.

Lily chose one of these numbers.

She divided it by 5. The answer was an odd number.

Malik could have chosen _____

or _____ .

Lily could have chosen _____ .

What do you notice? _____

_____ .

Reflect

Myra shares 35 grapes between 5 friends.

How many does each friend get?

Explain what method you would use to work the answer.

_____

_____

_____

_____

Dividing by 10

1 Pari is planting beans.

She plants rows of 10.

She has 40 seeds.

How many rows can she plant?

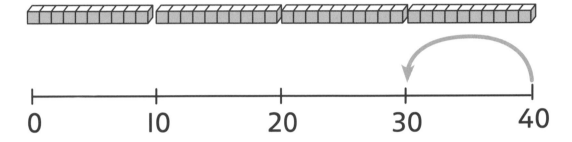

$40 \div 10 = \boxed{}$

She plants $\boxed{}$ rows.

2 Complete each number fact.

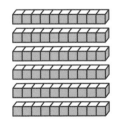

$60 \div 10 = \boxed{}$

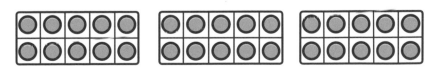

$30 \div 10 = \boxed{}$

$50 \div 10 = \boxed{}$

3 Draw lines to match the sentences, then complete them.

I know 3 × 10 = ☐

I know ☐ × 10 = 70

I know 4 × 10 = ☐

I know ☐ × 10 = 90

so 70 ÷ 10 = ☐

so 30 ÷ 10 = ☐

so 90 ÷ 10 = ☐

so ☐ ÷ 10 = 4

4 Complete each number fact.

40 ÷ 10 = ☐

60 ÷ 10 = ☐

☐ = 80 ÷ 10

70 ÷ 10 = ☐

☐ ÷ 10 = 9

20 ÷ 10 = ☐

☐ ÷ 10 = 1

☐ = 30 ÷ 10

☐ × 10 = 10

2 × ☐ = 20

3 × 10 = ☐

4 × 10 = 40

☐ × 10 = 50

6 × 10 = ☐

☐ × 10 = 70

8 × ☐ = 80

5 Try to crack the codes.

a) ⬜ × 10 = 30

⬜ + △ = 100

30 ÷ ⬜ = 10

? = ⬜

△? = ⬜

b) ⬜ × 10 = 70

⬜ + △ = 10

70 ÷ ⬜ = 10

? = ⬜

△? = ⬜

What do you notice?

Reflect

What division sentences can you write by using the 10 times-table?

$1 × 10 = 10$
$2 × 10 = 20$
$3 × 10 = 30$
$4 × 10 = 40$
$5 × 10 = 50$
$6 × 10 = 60$
$7 × 10 = 70$
$8 × 10 = 80$
$9 × 10 = 90$
$10 × 10 = 100$

→ Textbook 2B p32

Bar modelling – grouping

1 Sally has 14 shoes.

How many pairs are there?

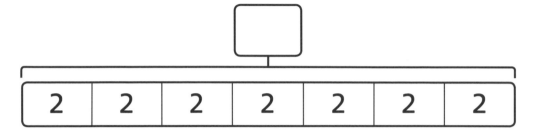

$14 \div 2 = \boxed{}$

There are $\boxed{}$ pairs.

2 Jamal makes a pattern using buttons.

Each pattern uses 5 buttons.

He has 40 buttons in total.

How many patterns can he make?

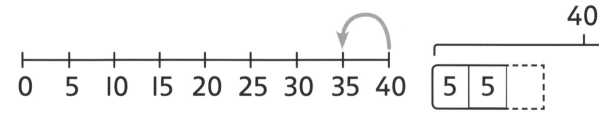

$40 \div 5 = \boxed{}$

Jamal can make $\boxed{}$ patterns.

24

3 Fill in the correct numbers and complete the sentences.

| 10 | 10 | 10 | 10 |

☐ ÷ ☐ = ☐

☐ is ☐ groups of ☐ .

| 2 | 2 | 2 | 2 | 2 |

☐ ÷ ☐ = ☐

☐ is ☐ groups of ☐ .

4 Match the picture to the bar model. Then match the picture to the right number sentence.

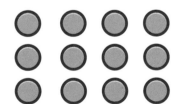

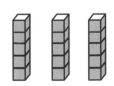

| 3 | 3 | 3 | 3 |

| 5 | 5 | 5 |

| 4 | 4 | 4 | 4 |

16 ÷ 4 = 4   15 ÷ 5 = 3   12 ÷ 3 = 4

5 Eva is working on a division question.

$\bigcirc \div 5 = \boxed{}$

5	5	

She completes the diagram.

There are an even number of bars.

What could $\bigcirc$ be? _____

Reflect

5	5	5	5

I will make it a grouping problem.

Invent a division problem to match this diagram.

_____

_____

_____

_____

_____

_____

Bar modelling – sharing

1 3 children need to carry 15 books to the library.

Share the books between the children.

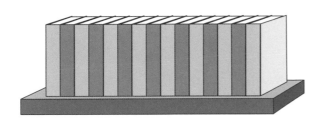

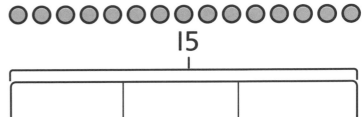

15

$15 \div \boxed{} = \boxed{}$

Each child carries $\boxed{}$ books.

2 There are 25 ⟍⟍⟍⟍ .

There are 20 ⟍⟍⟍ .

There are 10 ⟍⟍ .

5 tables of children share the brushes.

How many brushes does each table get?

	Table 1	Table 2	Table 3	Table 4	Table 5
⟍⟍⟍⟍					
⟍⟍⟍					
⟍⟍					

3 Complete the bar models and sentences.

Bani has 12 guinea pig treats.

Pavel has 12 rabbit treats.

Joe has 12 cat treats.

They share them equally among their pets.

How many treats does each pet get?

12

12 ÷ 4 = ☐

Each _____ gets 3 treats.

12

12 ÷ 6 = ☐

Each _____ gets ☐ treats.

12

12 ÷ 3 = ☐

Each _____ gets 4 treats.

4 5 children want a go on the trampoline before lunch.

They share the time equally for half an hour.

Draw a bar model to show how much time each child gets.

$$\boxed{} \div 5 = \boxed{}$$

Reflect

Describe a bar model for sharing 30 between 5.

Now describe a bar model for making groups of 5 from 30.

What is the same and what is different?

→ Textbook 2B p40

Solving word problems – division

 a) Meg needs 50 .

They come in packs of 10.

How many packs should she buy?

50

| 10 | |

$\boxed{} \div \boxed{} = \boxed{}$

Meg should buy $\boxed{}$ packs.

b) Malik spends £20 on 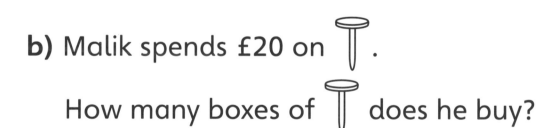.

How many boxes of does he buy?

£20

| £2 | |

$\boxed{} \div \boxed{} = \boxed{}$.

Malik buys $\boxed{}$ boxes of .

2 To make this stick person, you need
5 sticks and 1 counter.

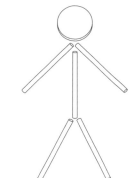

Roxy makes lots of these.

She uses 35 sticks.

How many counters does she need?

 ÷  =

She needs ☐ counters.

3 The money has to be shared between 8 people.

I don't think I can do that
because there are only 4 notes.

How much does each person get?

_____

_____

_____

4 There are fewer than 60 🍬 in a jar.

CHALLENGE

If the sweets were shared between 5 people, everyone would have an even number.

If the sweets were shared between 10 people, everyone would have an odd number.

How many sweets could there be?

Find 3 different solutions.

Reflect

Write your own word problem that is solved by 35 ÷ 5.

End of unit check

My journal

Which numbers give an odd answer when you divide by 5? Colour them blue.

Which numbers give an odd answer when you divide by 10? Colour them yellow.

Can you continue the pattern for the whole square?

Explain the patterns.

1	2	3	4	5	6	7	8	9	10
11	12	13	14	15	16	17	18	19	20
21	22	23	24	25	26	27	28	29	30
31	32	33	34	35	36	37	38	39	40
41	42	43	44	45	46	47	48	49	50
51	52	53	54	55	56	57	58	59	60
61	62	63	64	65	66	67	68	69	70
71	72	73	74	75	76	77	78	79	80
81	82	83	84	85	86	87	88	89	90
91	92	93	94	95	96	97	98	99	100

The pattern for blue is _____ .

This is because _____ .

The pattern for yellow is _____ .

This is because _____ .

These words might help you.

divide **odd**

even **ten**

digit **ones**

33

Power check

How do you feel about your work in this unit?

Power puzzle

Suki has 9 .

When she divides them into 2 equal piles there is 1 left over.

When she divides them into 3 piles there are none left over.

James has fewer than 50 .

When he makes towers of 2 there is 1  left over.

When he makes towers of 3 there is 1  left over.

When he makes towers of 4 there is 1  left over.

How many does he have?

→ Textbook 2B p48

Making tally charts

1 A group of children were asked to pick their favourite pet animal.

a) Complete the table.

Animal	Tally	Number
cat	ЖЖ ЖЖ ЖЖ IIII	
dog	ЖЖ ЖЖ ЖЖ II	
hamster	ЖЖ ЖЖ III	
fish	ЖЖ ЖЖ I	

b) Which animal was the most popular? _____

Which animal was the least popular? _____

How many more people chose dog than hamster?

2 Children in Year 2 were asked about their favourite sport.

Complete the tally chart to show the results.

Sport	Tally	Number
football		
rugby		
tennis		
cricket		

3 Complete the table. Then write three statements about the information.

CHALLENGE

Pizza toppings	Tally	Number
vegetables	ⅣⅢ ⅣⅢ ⅣⅢ ‖	17
chicken		19
meat feast	ⅣⅢ ⅣⅢ ‖‖	
cheese		13
mushroom	ⅣⅢ ‖	7

1 More people prefer _____ to _____ .

2 _____ .

3 _____ .

Reflect

As a class, complete a tally chart about your favourite subject in school.

→ Textbook 2B p52

Creating pictograms **❶**

❶

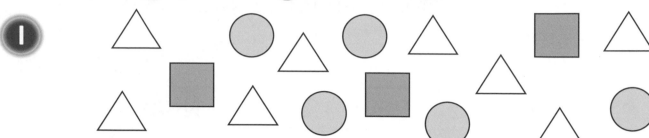

a) Tally these shapes.

Shape	Tally	Number
⬤		
◼		
△		

b) Draw a pictogram for the shapes.

Each ✖ represents I shape.

Shape	Number
circle	
square	
triangle	

2 Draw a pictogram for this tally chart.

Each ☐ represents I leaf.

Leaf	Tally
ash 🍃	IIII
beech 🍂	II
birch 🍃	III
oak 🍂	IIII III

Leaf	Number
ash 🍃	
beech 🍂	
birch 🍃	
oak 🍂	

3 Match the tally charts to the pictograms.

Each ⚽ represents I goal.

Name	Tally
Sandy	IIII II
Ravi	II
Liv	IIII I

Name	Number of goals
Sandy	⚽ ⚽ ⚽ ⚽ ⚽ ⚽
Ravi	⚽ ⚽
Liv	⚽ ⚽ ⚽ ⚽ ⚽

Name	Tally
Sandy	IIII I
Ravi	II
Liv	IIII

Name	Number of goals
Sandy	⚽ ⚽
Ravi	⚽ ⚽ ⚽ ⚽ ⚽ ⚽
Liv	⚽ ⚽ ⚽ ⚽ ⚽ ⚽

Name	Tally
Sandy	II
Ravi	IIII I
Liv	IIII I

Name	Number of goals
Sandy	⚽ ⚽ ⚽ ⚽ ⚽ ⚽ ⚽
Ravi	⚽ ⚽
Liv	⚽ ⚽ ⚽ ⚽ ⚽ ⚽

39

4 There are 25 children in Class A.

Here is part of a pictogram showing their favourite sports.

The rest of the children like tennis.

Complete the pictogram.

CHALLENGE

Sport	Number of children
rugby 🏉	🧍🧍🧍🧍🧍🧍🧍🧍
football ⚽	🧍🧍🧍🧍🧍🧍🧍🧍🧍🧍
tennis 🎾	

Each 🧍 represents I child.

Reflect

Use the given words to tell your friend how to complete a pictogram.

draw   make   match   count

- First, _____ the tally marks.

- Next, _____ pictures to _____ the tally marks.

- Finally, _____ a key.

Creating pictograms ❷

1 **a)** Jack has four types of sticker.

Complete the tally chart.

Sticker	Tally	Number
sun ☼		
smiley face ☺		
rainbow 🌈		
star ⭐		

b) Complete the pictogram to show Jack's stickers.

Each ◯ represents **2** stickers.

Sticker	Number of stickers
sun ☼	
smiley face ☺	
rainbow 🌈	
star ⭐	

2 Match the tally charts to the pictograms.

Each ☼ represents 10 days.

Weather	Tally
sunny	ⵜⵜⵜ ⵜⵜⵜ
cloudy	ⵜⵜⵜ I
rain	ⵜⵜⵜ ⵜⵜⵜ ⵜⵜⵜ

Weather	Number of days
sunny	☼
cloudy	☼
rain	☼ ☼

Each ☼ represents 2 days.

Weather	Tally
sunny	ⵜⵜⵜ ⵜⵜⵜ
cloudy	ⵜⵜⵜ
rain	ⵜⵜⵜ ⵜⵜⵜ ⵜⵜⵜ ⵜⵜⵜ

Weather	Number of days
sunny	☼ ☼ ☼ ☼ ☼
cloudy	☼ ☼ ☼
rain	☼ ☼ ☼ ☼ ☼ ☼ ☼ ☼

Each ☼ represents 5 days.

Weather	Tally
sunny	ⵜⵜⵜ ⵜⵜⵜ
cloudy	ⵜⵜⵜ
rain	ⵜⵜⵜ ⵜⵜⵜ ⵜⵜⵜ

Weather	Number of days
sunny	☼ ☼
cloudy	☼
rain	☼ ☼ ☼

3 Use the clues to complete the pictogram.

CHALLENGE

Each ⚽ represents 10 goals.

Goals scored	Number
Kira	⚽ ⚽
Hassan	
Alfie	
Lola	

Alfie scored double the number of goals to Kira.

Lola scored 10 more goals than Alfie.

Hassan scored half as many goals as Lola.

Reflect

100 children are asked who their favourite author is. There are five authors to choose from.

Tick the best key to use. Explain your answer.

📖 = 1 child	📖 = 5 children	📖 = 10 children

_____

_____

→ Textbook 2B p60

Interpreting pictograms ❶

1 Complete the tally chart to match the pictogram.

Each  represents 1 medal.

Medal colour	Number won
gold	🏅🏅🏅🏅🏅🏅🏅🏅🏅🏅🏅🏅🏅
silver	🏅🏅🏅🏅🏅🏅🏅
bronze	🏅🏅🏅🏅🏅🏅🏅🏅🏅🏅🏅

Medal colour	Tally
gold	
silver	
bronze	

a) How many gold medals were won?

b) How many silver and bronze medals were won altogether?

c) How many more gold medals were won than silver medals?

> I will use the tally chart to tell me how many there are of each medal.

2 Look at the pictogram.

Each ✿ represents I flower.

Flower	Number
daisy	✿ ✿ ✿ ✿ ✿ ✿ ✿ ✿ ✿
sunflower	✿ ✿ ✿ ✿ ✿ ✿ ✿ ✿ ✿ ✿ ✿
poppy	✿ ✿ ✿ ✿ ✿ ✿ ✿ ✿
tulip	✿ ✿ ✿ ✿ ✿ ✿
daffodil	✿ ✿ ✿ ✿ ✿ ✿ ✿ ✿ ✿ ✿ ✿ ✿

a) Complete the sentences.

There are ☐ more daisies than tulips.

There are ☐ fewer poppies than sunflowers.

There are 2 fewer _____ than sunflowers.

b) How many flowers are there altogether? ☐

c) Sid chose two different flowers from the pictogram.

He has 20 flowers altogether.

Which two flowers could Sid have chosen?

Can you find more than one option?

_____

_____

Reflect

Ice cream	Number
vanilla	🍦🍦🍦🍦🍦
strawberry	🍦🍦🍦
chocolate	🍦🍦🍦🍦🍦🍦🍦

What is wrong with this pictogram?

_____

_____

_____

_____

Interpreting pictograms ❷

1 Zeb and Tilly are on a journey.

They count different vehicles.

| Each ◎ represents 2 vehicles. |

Vehicle	Number
car	◎ ◎ ◎ ◎ ◎ ◎
lorry	◎ ◎
van	◎ ◎ ◎ ◎
motorbike	◎ ◎ ◎ ◎ ◎

a) How many cars do they see? ☐

b) How many more vans do they see than

lorries? ☐

c) How many motorbikes do they see? ☐

d) How many vehicles do they see altogether? ☐

e) Zeb says, 'We saw four more cars than lorries.'

Is Zeb correct? _____

2

Each 👤 represents 2 children.

	Class 1
boys	👤👤👤👤👤👤👤👤
girls	👤👤👤👤👤👤👤

	Class 2
boys	👤👤👤👤👤👤👤
girls	👤👤👤👤👤👤👤👤👤

a) Which class has more boys?

b) How many more girls are in Class 2 than in Class 1?

c) How many boys are there in total?

3 Lottie counts how many buses are seen on each bus route near her house.

Complete the pictogram so that 1  represents 5 buses.

 = 10 buses		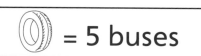 = 5 buses

route 1	🛞🛞🛞
route 2	🛞🛞
route 3	🛞🛞
route 4	🛞🛞🛞

route 1	
route 2	
route 3	
route 4	

CHALLENGE

Reflect

Which pictogram would you use to show the favourite sweet? Why?

✳ = 10 sweets	
chew	✳ ✳
lollipop	✳ ✳ ✳
chocolate	✳ ✳ ✳ ✳
marshmallow	✳ ✳ ✳ ✳

✳ = 2 sweets	
chew	✳ ✳ ✳ ✳ ✳ ✳ ✳ ✳ ✳
lollipop	✳ ✳ ✳ ✳ ✳ ✳ ✳ ✳ ✳ ✳ ✳ ✳
chocolate	✳ ✳ ✳ ✳ ✳ ✳ ✳ ✳ ✳ ✳ ✳ ✳ ✳ ✳
marshmallow	✳ ✳ ✳ ✳ ✳ ✳ ✳ ✳ ✳ ✳ ✳ ✳ ✳ ✳

_____

_____

_____

_____

→ Textbook 2B p68

Block diagrams

1 The block diagram shows how many times children played on equipment at the park.

a) Which was the most popular equipment?

_____

b) Which was the least popular equipment?

_____

c) How many times were the [swings] used? ☐

d) How many more times was the [slide] used than the [horse] ? ☐

25					
24					
23					
22					
21					
20			■		
19			■		
18	■		■		
17	■		■		
16	■	■	■		■
15	■	■	■		■
14	■	■	■		■
13	■	■	■		■
12	■	■	■		■
11	■	■	■		■
10	■	■	■		■
9	■	■	■		■
8	■	■	■		■
7	■	■	■		■
6	■	■	■		■
5	■	■	■		■
4	■	■	■		■
3	■	■	■	■	■
2	■	■	■	■	■
1	■	■	■	■	■
	Swings	Slide	Climbing frame	Horse	Roundabout

2 Children in Year 2 were asked their favourite fruit.

Use the information to complete the block diagram.

 16 8

 7 12

 14

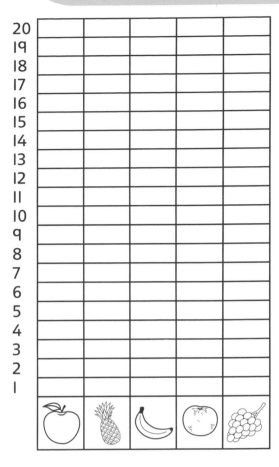

3 Children in Year 2 were asked about their holidays.

a) How many children said

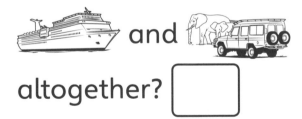 and

altogether? ☐

b) How many more children said

 than  ? ☐

c) Circle the third most popular holiday on the block diagram.

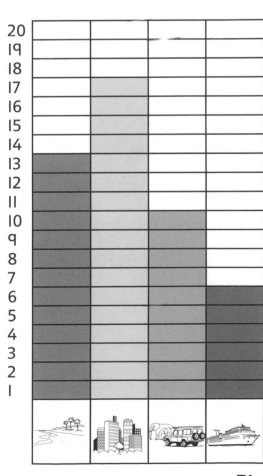

What mistakes can you see?

```
15
14
13
12
10
 9
 8
 7
 6
 5
 4
 3
 2
 1
```

_____

_____

Reflect

Explain why a block diagram would not be a helpful way to represent these numbers.

75   80   27

_____

_____

Solving word problems

1 The diagrams show how 30 children get to school.

Transport	Tally	Number
car		8
bike	ⵑ|	
walk		9
bus	ⵑ||	

Block diagram (y-axis 1 to 10): car, bike, walk, bus

a) Complete the tally chart and the block diagram.

b) How many more children walk than take the bus?

c) Complete this pictogram to show the same information.

◯ represents 2 children.

Transport	Number
car	
bike	
walk	
bus	

53

2 Steve is tallying letters in a word.

Letter	Tally
B	/
E	⫽⫽⫽⫽
K	/
P	/
R	/

It is someone who looks after buzzing insects!

What is Steve's word?

3 **a)** Use the information to complete each diagram of favourite t-shirt colours.

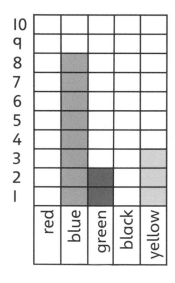

Colour	Number
red	🧺🧺🧺
blue	🧺🧺🧺🧺
green	
black	
yellow	🧺🧺

Colour	Tally	Number
red	⫽⫽⫽⫽	
blue		
green	//	
black	⫽⫽⫽⫽ //	
yellow		

b) What is the value of each 🧺 ?

🧺 = [ ] t-shirts

4 This is a pictogram of favourite 🍦 flavours. **CHALLENGE**

Each 🍦 represents 1 vote.

strawberry	🍦🍦🍦🍦🍦🍦🍦🍦🍦
vanilla	🍦🍦🍦🍦🍦🍦🍦
chocolate	🍦🍦🍦🍦🍦

Draw another pictogram for the same information.

This time each 🍦 = 2 votes.

Each 🍦 represents 2 votes.

strawberry	
vanilla	
chocolate	

Reflect

Which chart or diagram do you prefer to use? Why?

_____

_____

_____

_____

→ Textbook 2B p76

End of unit check

My journal

Each  represents 5 cars.

blue	🚐 🚐 🚐 🚐 🚐
red	🚐 🚐 🚐 🚐
yellow	🚐 🚐
purple	🚐 🚐 🚐 🚐

Today I saw more purple cars than red cars.

Is Ola correct? Explain your answer.

- _____
- _____

Create your own sentences about this pictogram.

- _____
- _____

These words might help you.

equal   **more than**

less than   **most**

least   **same as**

difference   **total**

56

Power check

How do you feel about your work in this unit?

Power puzzle

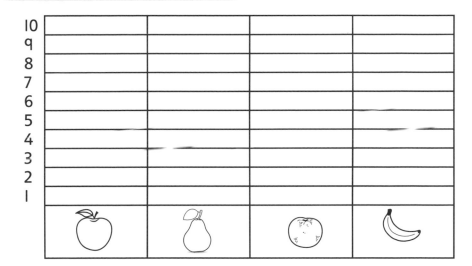

A box contains some fruit.

Try to work out how many of each fruit are in the box.

- There are 25 pieces of fruit in total.
- There are twice as many apples as pears.
- There are 2 more oranges than pears.
- There are 3 bananas.
- There are 10 apples.

Complete the block diagram to show this.

→ Textbook 2B p80

Measuring in centimetres

1 Complete the sentences.

a)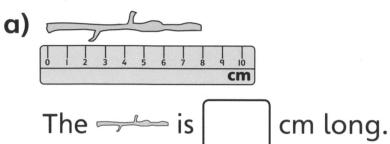

The ⚊ is ☐ cm long.

> These rulers are not real rulers, so the centimetres are not quite the correct length.

b)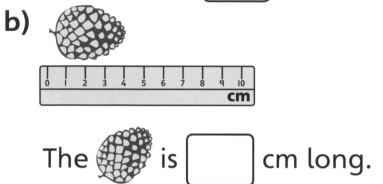

The 🌰 is ☐ cm long.

c) Draw something shorter than ⚊ but longer than the 🌰.

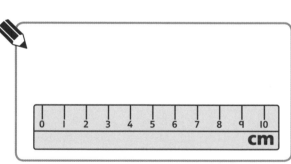

2 Complete the sentences.

a)  The 🍄 is ☐ cm tall.

b)  The 🪶 is ☐ cm long.

c) ☐ cm is greater than ☐ cm.

3 Use a ruler to draw a snail trail that is:

a) 7 cm long

b) 10 cm long

c) between 12 cm and 19 cm long.

4 Find objects to complete the table. Use a ruler.

Length	Objects I have found
Less than 10 cm	
10 cm	
15 cm	
26 cm	
Greater than 30 cm	

I wonder how I can measure something longer than 30 cm with a 30 cm ruler.

5 True or false? Explain why.

a)

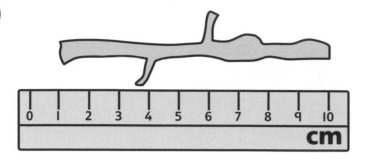

The stick is 10 cm long.

_____

_____

b)

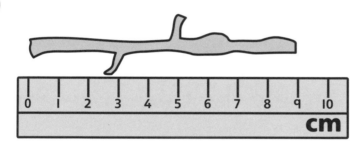

The stick is 9 cm long.

_____

_____

Reflect

Draw a line using a ruler.

Ask your partner to measure it.

Are they correct?

Measuring in metres

1 Look at items around your classroom. Complete the table.

Less than 1 metre	Equal to 1 metre	Greater than 1 metre

If something is longer or taller than my metre stick, which column shall I put it in?

2 Measure these items in your school:

a) The length of the school hall is about [   ].

b) The length of a school bench is about [   ].

c) The height of my classroom door is about [   ].

I wonder why doors are taller than they are long.

3 Match the items to the measures.

2 metres   30 cm   5 cm   20 metres

4 Tick centimetres or metres.

a) My classroom is about

6 centimetres ☐ long.

6 metres ☐

b) My chair is about

90 centimetres ☐ tall.

90 metres ☐

c) My pencil is about

20 centimetres ☐ long.

20 metres ☐

d) My desk is about

1 centimetre ☐ wide.

1 metre ☐

I know that 1 centimetre is less than 1 metre.

5 What do you think might be 2 metres long?

CHALLENGE

Reflect

What would you use a metre stick to measure?

What would you use a 30 cm ruler to measure?

→ Textbook 2B p88

Comparing lengths

1 Tick the longer total distance.

a)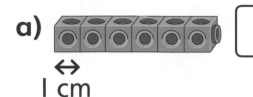

↔
l cm

b)

l m

c) 45 m ☐ 44 m ☐

2 A bin is 52 cm tall. A stool is 48 cm tall.

Which is taller?

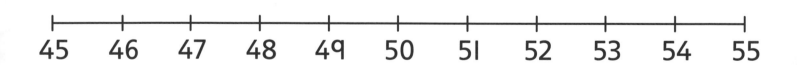

45   46   47   48   49   50   51   52   53   54   55

52 ◯ 48

The _____ is taller than the _____ .

3 Use < or > to make the statements true.

a) 37 cm ◯ 73 cm

b) 90 m ◯ 30 m

c) 15 cm ◯ 15 m

d) 65 m ◯ 75 m

e) 65 m ◯ 85m

f) 65 m ◯ 95m

4 Complete the statements to make them true.

a) 3 ☐ cm > 34 cm

b) 50 m < ☐ 9 m

c) 11 m > 1 ☐ cm

d) ☐ 6 cm = 3 ☐ cm

e) ☐ 8 cm > ☐ 9 cm

Compare your answers with your partner.

65

5 Which is longer?

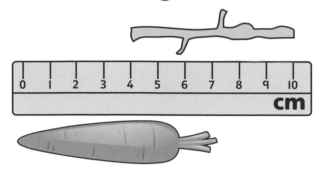

The _____ is longer.

6 Jay thinks that 20 cm is less than I m.

Do you agree? Explain why.

_____

_____

Reflect

Measure your book and your pencil.

Which is longer?

_____

_____

_____

Ordering lengths

1 Order each jump from shortest to longest.

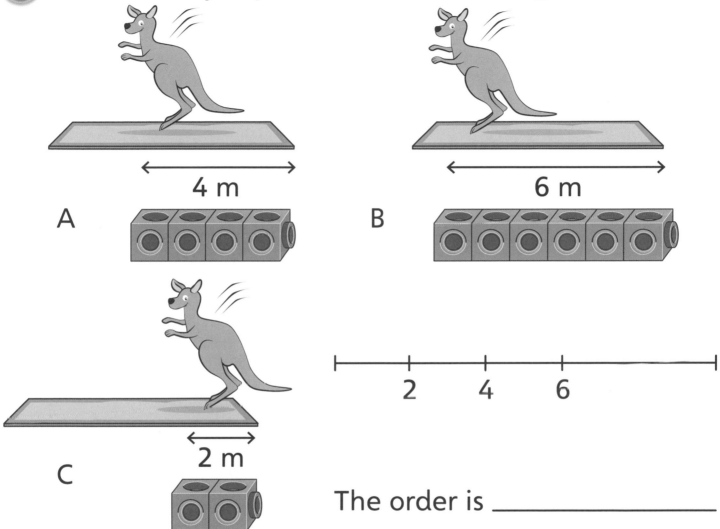

The order is _____

2 Measure each line. Put them in order from shortest to longest.

a)

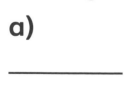

b)

c)

d)

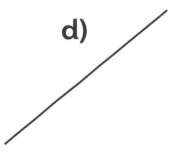

The order is _____

3 Order the numbers from smallest to greatest.

a) 53 cm, 40 cm, 44 cm

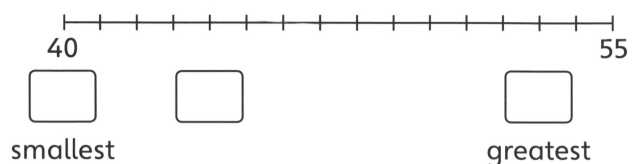

smallest		greatest

b) 27 m, 55 m, 31 m

Tens	Ones

Tens	Ones

Tens	Ones

smallest   greatest

4 Change one number so each set is correct.

a)

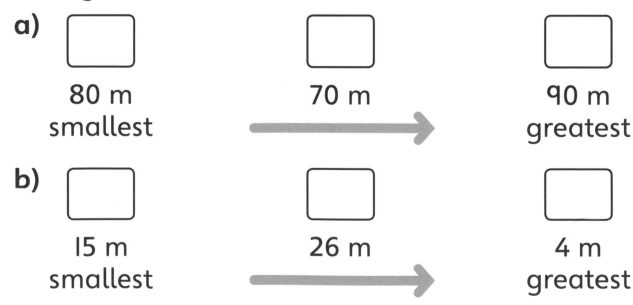

80 m
smallest

70 m

90 m
greatest

b)

15 m
smallest

26 m

4 m
greatest

68

5 Choose a number for each box.

a) 35 m   12 m   [ ]

greatest ⟶   smallest

b) [ ]   49 cm   41 cm

greatest ⟶   smallest

c) 20 m   18 m   [ ]

greatest ⟶   smallest

Reflect

Roll a dice twice to make a 2-digit length in metres.
Record it in a place value grid.

Tens	Ones

36 metres

Roll the dice to make two more 2-digit lengths.
Choose a way to order them.

→ Textbook 2B p96

Solving word problems – length

1 **a)** Zara is 90 cm tall.

Her younger brother Ellis is 60 cm tall.

How much taller is Zara than Ellis?

Zara is ⬜ cm taller than Ellis.

b) Zara's leg is 41 cm long.

Ellis's leg is 27 cm long.

How much shorter is Ellis's leg than Zara's leg?

Ellis's leg is ⬜ cm shorter than Zara's leg.

2 **a)** If a badger is 70 cm long and a fox is 18 cm shorter, then the fox is ☐ cm long.

b) If a sheep is 96 cm tall and a dog is 28 cm shorter, then the dog is ☐ cm tall.

3 **a)** A 20 cm long strip of paper has been cut into two equal pieces.

Each piece of paper is ☐ cm long.

b) A strip of paper has been cut into four equal pieces. Each piece is 5 cm long.

The strip of paper was ☐ cm long.

4 Tom is running 100 metres.

He runs 40 metres.

He runs another 36 metres.

How much does he still have to run?

CHALLENGE

First I

Then

Tom has [ ] m still to run.

Reflect

A snake is 30 cm long.
Another snake is 58 cm long.
What is the total length of the snakes?

Explain your steps.

End of unit check

My journal

The pencil is 8 cm long.

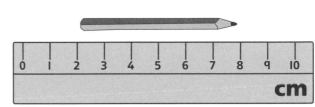

Is Hassan correct? Explain your answer.

_____

_____

_____

_____

These words might help you.

ruler

centimetre   **metre**

long   **short**   **tall**

Power check

How do you feel about your work in this unit?

Power play

How many ways can you use objects from your classroom to show your partner a metre?

You will need:
- a metre stick
- objects from your classroom

I used two pens, two maths books and a water bottle to make I metre.

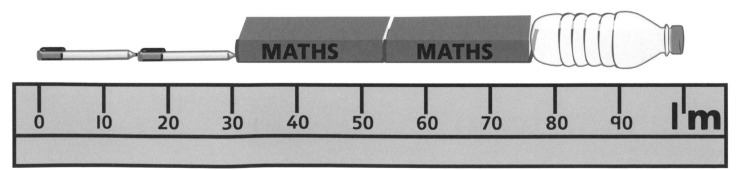

Recognising 2D and 3D shapes

1 **a)** Colour in all the triangles.

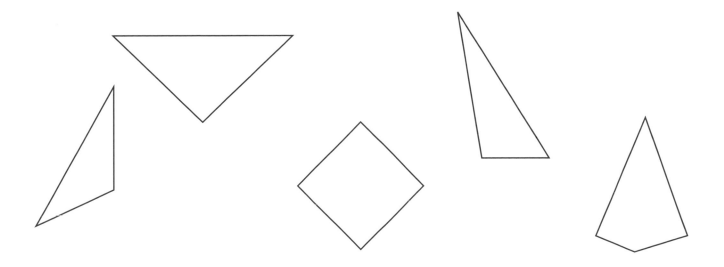

b) Colour in all the squares.

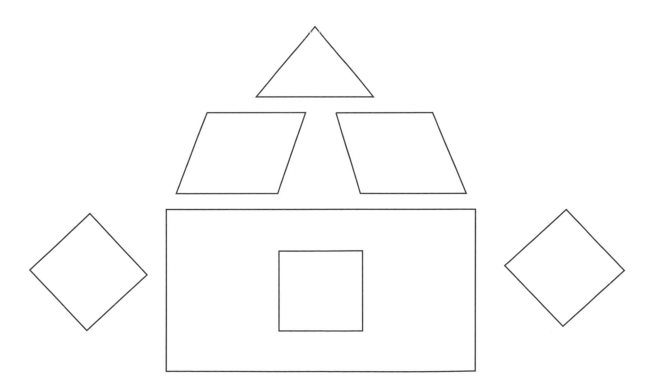

2 How many cuboids, pyramids and spheres are there in this picture?

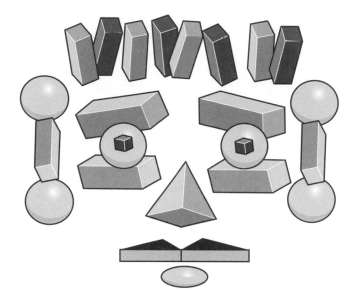

There are ⬚ cuboids.

There are ⬚ pyramids.

There are ⬚ spheres.

3 Sara and Ibrahim are drawing around 3D shapes.

Write the name of the 2D shape each child will draw.

Sara will draw a _____ .

Ibrahim will draw a _____ .

4 Children made pictures by sticking shapes on paper.

Match each child to their picture.

I used an odd number of rectangles.

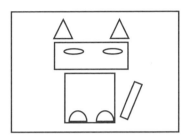

I used an even number of triangles.

I used no circles.

Mine has more than one square.

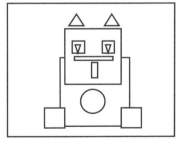

Reflect

Name three 2D shapes and three 3D shapes.

Point to them in the classroom or on the page.

→ Textbook 2B p108

Drawing 2D shapes

1 These are the dots for the corners of polygons.

Complete each polygon.

One has been done for you.

Write the name of each shape.

Use a ruler to join the dots.

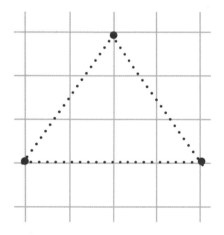

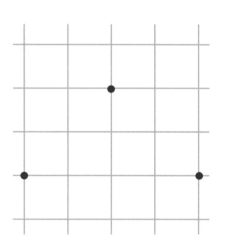

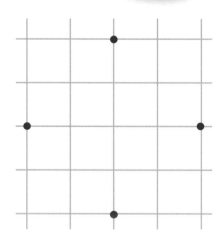

_____

_____

_____

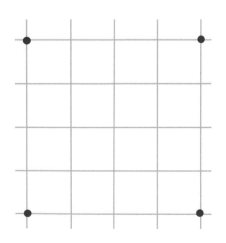

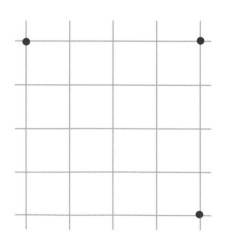

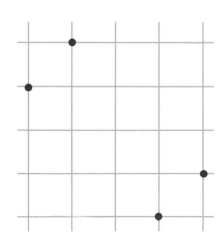

_____

_____

_____

2 Draw one more dot for each rectangle, then complete each shape.

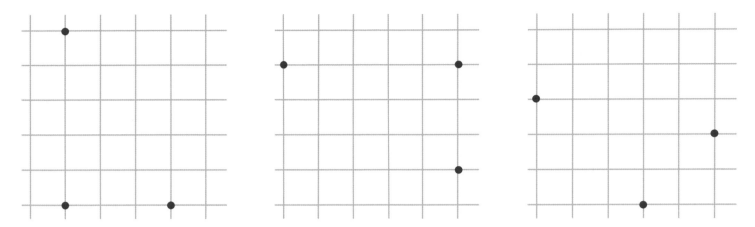

3 Copy the triangles from the square grid to the plain paper.

One has been started for you.

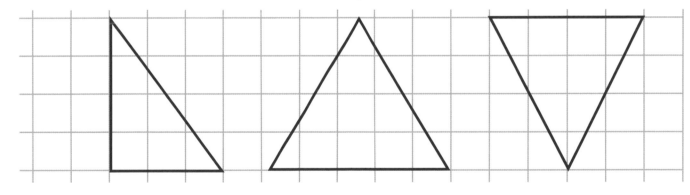

4 How many different squares can you draw on these grids?

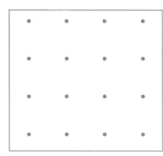
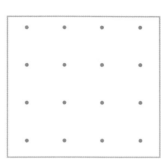

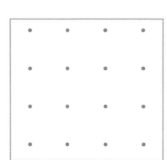
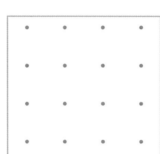
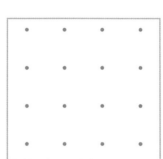

Reflect

Give three instructions for how to draw this shape accurately.

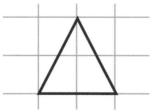

First, _____.

Then, _____.

Finally, _____.

Counting sides on 2D shapes

1 Complete the table.

Shape	Name	Number of sides
	tri_ng_e	
	pent_g_n	
	_ _ _ _ _ r e	
	r_c_a_g_e	4
	hex_g_n	

2 Match the shape to the sentence.

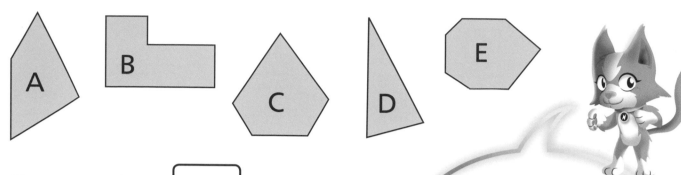

Shape D has ☐ sides.

Shape A has ☐ sides.

There is one sentence for each shape.

Shape ____ has more than six sides.

Shape ____ has five sides.

Shape ____ has an even number of sides.

3 Complete the drawings.

How many sides does each shape have?

A   B   C   D

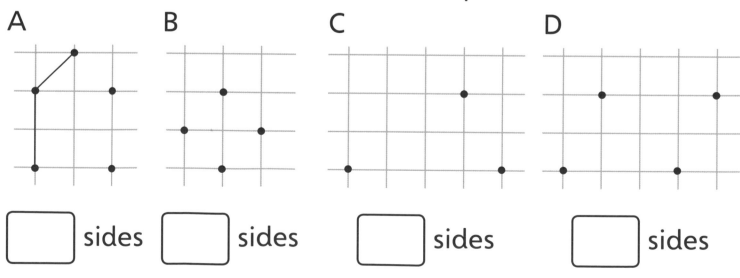

☐ sides   ☐ sides   ☐ sides   ☐ sides

CHALLENGE

4 **a)** Rob makes five triangles.

To make five triangles,

he needs ☐ sticks.

b) Isla makes five pentagons.

To make five pentagons, she needs ☐ sticks.

c) Jasmine uses 12 sticks. She makes three shapes.
What shapes could she have made?

They could all be the same, or all be different.

Reflect

Which shape is the odd one out? Why?

→ Textbook 2B p116

Counting vertices on 2D shapes

1 Match the shapes to the number of vertices.

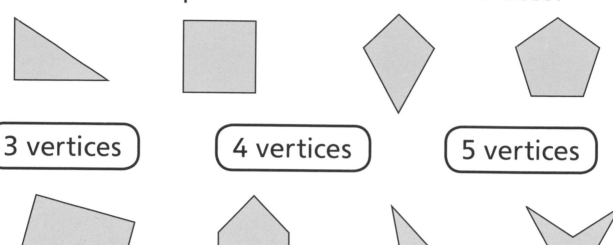

3 vertices   4 vertices   5 vertices

2 Complete the table.

Shape	Number of vertices

84

3 Complete the sentences with the words below.

Use each word once.

square   pentagon   hexagon   triangle   rectangle

A _____ has five vertices and five sides.

A shape with four vertices could be a _____ or a _____ .

A _____ has fewer vertices than a square.

Every shape with six vertices is called a _____ .

4

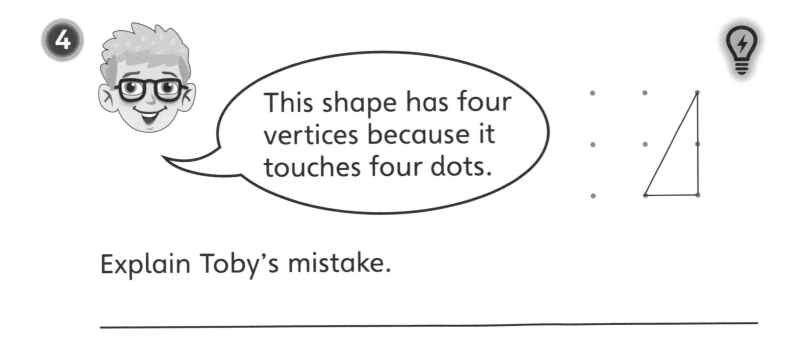

This shape has four vertices because it touches four dots.

Explain Toby's mistake.

_____

_____

85

5 Draw two different shapes with four vertices.

Draw two different shapes with five vertices.

Reflect

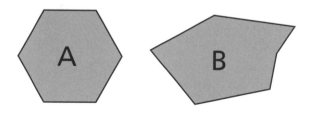

It's easy to count the vertices on shape A. It's harder to count the vertices on shape B.

Explain what is the same and what is different.

Think about where the vertices are.

Finding lines of symmetry

1 Draw a line of symmetry on each of these shapes.

2 Complete the symmetrical shapes.

a)

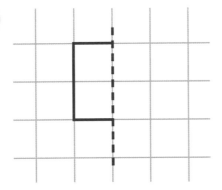

c)

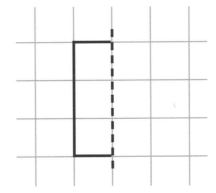

b)

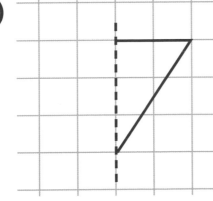

d)

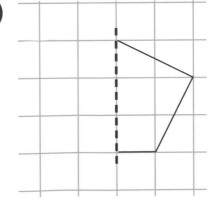

3 Match the folded shapes to the whole shapes.

4 Tick or cross each shape to show whether the line of symmetry is correct.

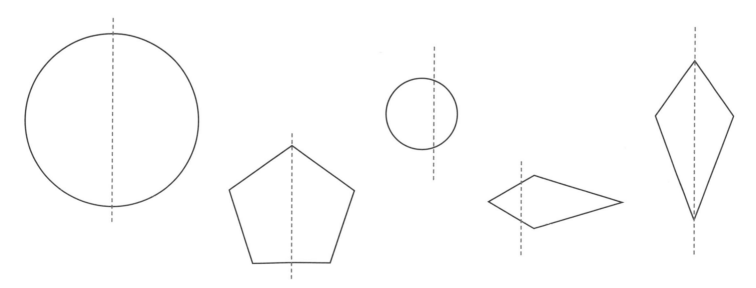

5 Draw half a shape that would unfold to be a quadrilateral.

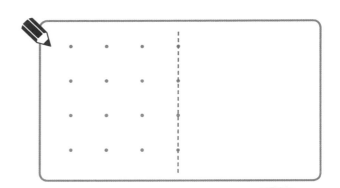

6 Make a symmetrical shape by folding and cutting a piece of paper.

Draw it here and show the line of symmetry.

Reflect

I have a shape. It has fewer than five vertices. It is symmetrical.

Explain to your partner what this shape could look like.

Now draw the shape.

→ Textbook 2B p124

Sorting 2D shapes

1 Match each shape to the correct group.

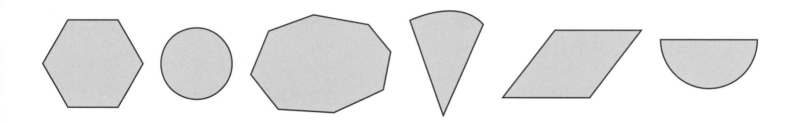

2 Sort these shapes into order by number of vertices, from the fewest number of vertices to the most.

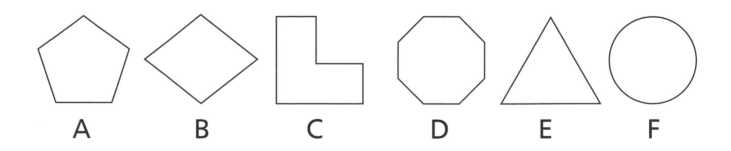

A　　B　　C　　D　　E　　F

Fewest _____ Most

3 Write labels for these groups.

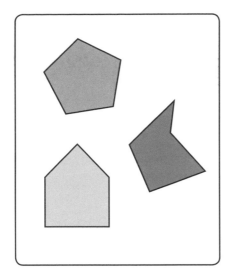 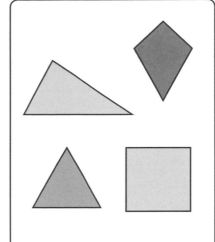 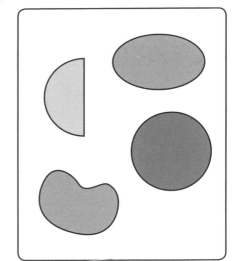

_____   _____   _____

4 Draw two different shapes to go in each group.

Odd number of vertices   Even number of vertices

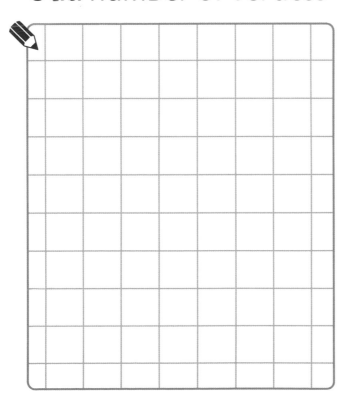 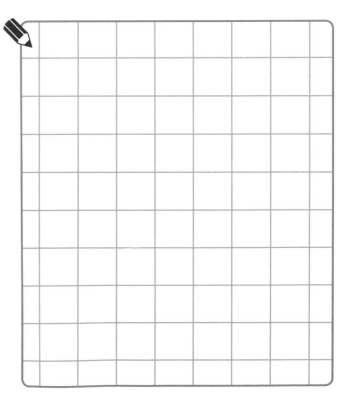

5 **a)** Draw two different shapes, one that could go in each group.

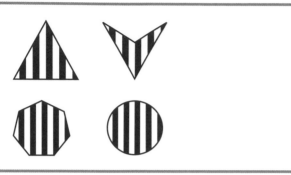

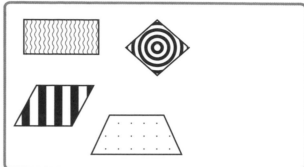

b) Draw a shape that could go in both groups.

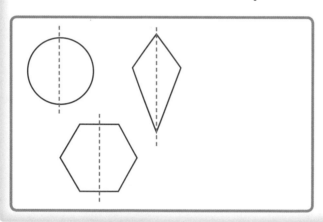

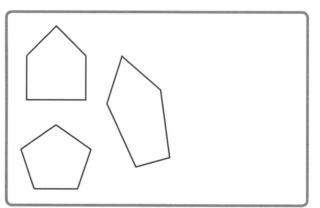

Reflect

Explain how you could sort these shapes into two groups so each group has the same number of shapes in it.

Making patterns with 2D shapes

1 Show the repeating part of each pattern.

The first one has been done for you.

a)

b)

c)

d)

2 Circle the shapes that complete the patterns.

a)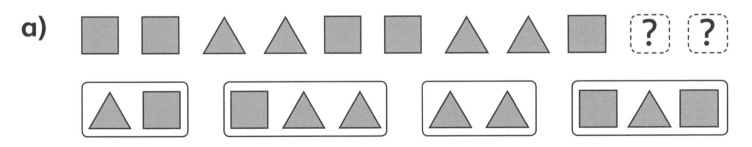

b)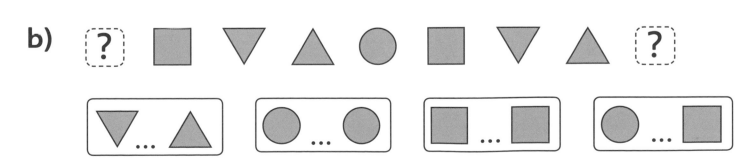

3 Draw the shapes that would be in 10th position and 20th position for each pattern.

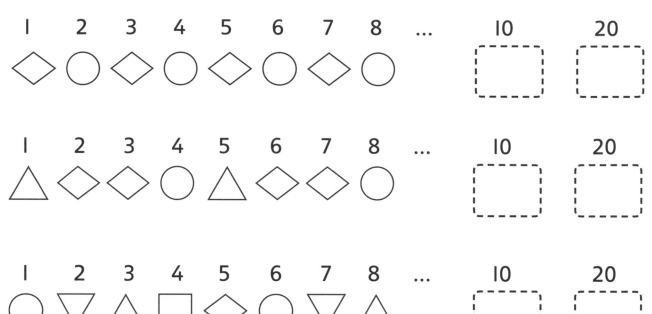

4 Draw the next four shapes.

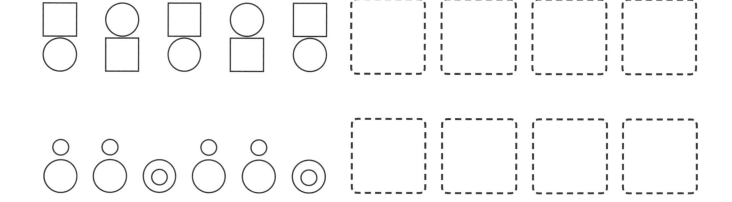

5 Complete these grids by following the patterns.

CHALLENGE

a)

b)

Reflect

Design your own pattern question for this game.

Complete the pattern using one of these options.

A:

C:

B:

D:

95

→ Textbook 2B p132

Counting faces on 3D shapes

1 Complete the table.

Shape	Name	Number of faces
	_u_e	
	p_r_m_d	
	cu_oi_	
	py_a_ _d	
	s_ _e_e	0

2 Match each 3D shape to its faces

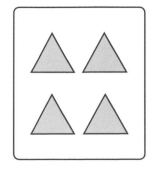 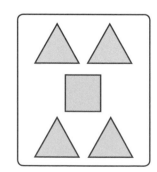 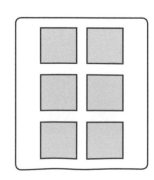 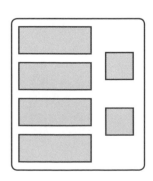

3 Write the letters of the shapes each child could have.

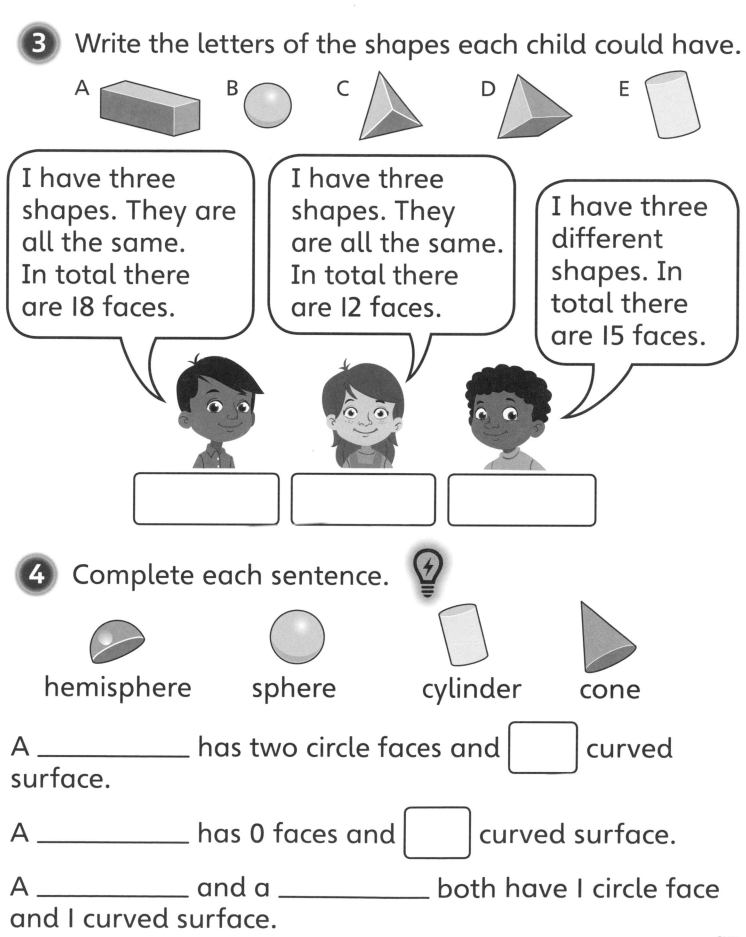

A   B   C   D   E

I have three shapes. They are all the same. In total there are 18 faces.

I have three shapes. They are all the same. In total there are 12 faces.

I have three different shapes. In total there are 15 faces.

4 Complete each sentence.

hemisphere   sphere   cylinder   cone

A _____ has two circle faces and ☐ curved surface.

A _____ has 0 faces and ☐ curved surface.

A _____ and a _____ both have I circle face and I curved surface.

97

5 **a)**

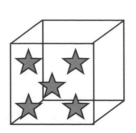 

CHALLENGE

Ned puts five stickers on each face of this cube.

How many stickers does he need in total?

Ned needs ☐ stickers.

b)

Sophie puts four stickers on each face of her shape.

She uses eight stickers in total.

Which shape did she use?

She used the _____ .

Reflect

Name a 3D shape.

Challenge your partner to tell you the shape of its faces.

Then ask your partner to challenge you in the same way.

Counting edges on 3D shapes

1 How many edges does each shape have?

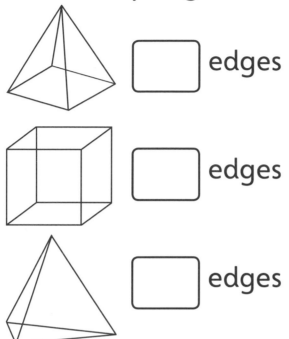

☐ edges

☐ edges

☐ edges

2 Use the clues to write the correct letter on each label.

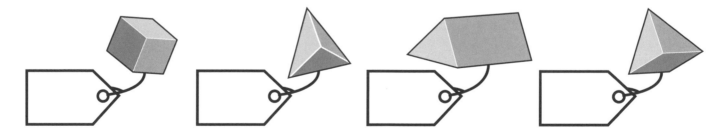

Shape A has an odd number of edges.

Shape B has the most edges.

Shape C has four fewer edges than a cuboid.

Shape D is on the right of the cuboid.

3 Complete the sentences.

cube   triangular prism   square-based pyramid

A _____ has 6 faces and 12 edges.

A _____ has 5 faces and 9 edges.

A _____ has 5 faces and 8 edges.

4 Not all prisms have triangular ends.

Complete the sketch and write the number of edges for each.

A pentagonal prism has ☐ edges.

A hexagonal prism has ☐ edges.

This prism has ☐ edges.

This prism has ☐ edges.

CHALLENGE

5 **a)** Maddy made five △ using ┃.

How many ┃ did she use in total?

Maddy used ☐ ┃.

b) Gabriel used 50 sticks to make △.

How many did he make?

Gabriel made ☐ △.

Reflect

Explain the difference between a face and an edge of a 3D shape.

→ **Textbook 2B p140**

Counting vertices on 3D shapes

1 Complete the table.

Shape	Number of vertices
▲	
●	
◢	

I count vertices where edges meet.

2 Complete these sentences.

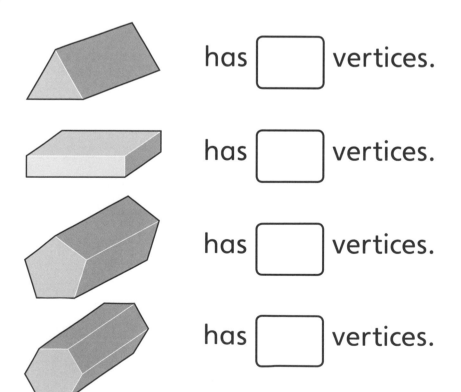

has ☐ vertices.

has ☐ vertices.

has ☐ vertices.

has ☐ vertices.

3 Match the shapes to the number of vertices.

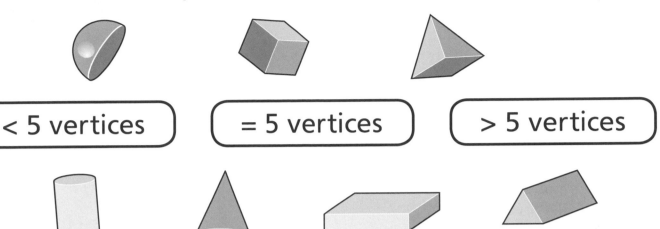

| < 5 vertices | = 5 vertices | > 5 vertices |

4 **a)** Will has 20 marshmallows.

He makes two different shapes.
He has six marshmallows left.

Circle the shapes he has made.

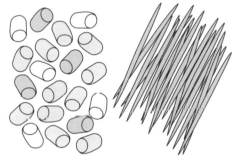

b) Rose has 20 marshmallows.

She makes three different shapes. She has three marshmallows left.

Circle the shapes she has made.

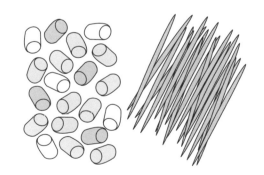

 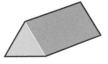

5 Complete the drawings for these pyramids. **CHALLENGE**

Write the number of faces, edges and vertices for each one.

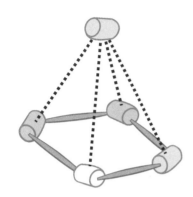 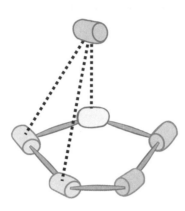 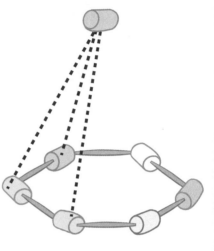

Faces = ☐   Faces = ☐   Faces = ☐

Edges = ☐   Edges = ☐   Edges = ☐

Vertices = ☐   Vertices = ☐   Vertices = ☐

Reflect

What is your favourite 3D shape? _____

How many vertices does it have? ☐

Compare with other people on your table.

Sorting 3D shapes

1 Circle the shapes that are in the wrong place.

Has a curved surface

Has more than one square face

Has fewer than five vertices

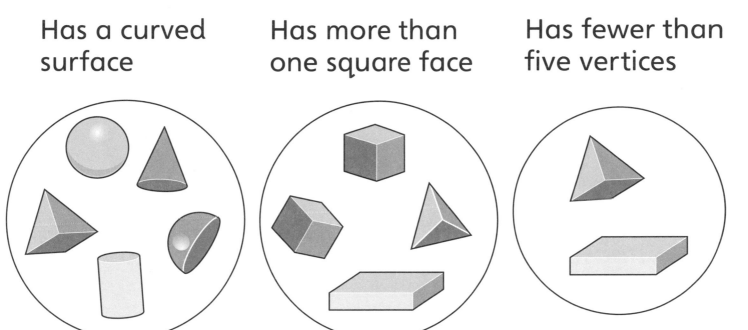

2 Tick the shape that could go in both groups.

Odd number of faces

Even number of edges

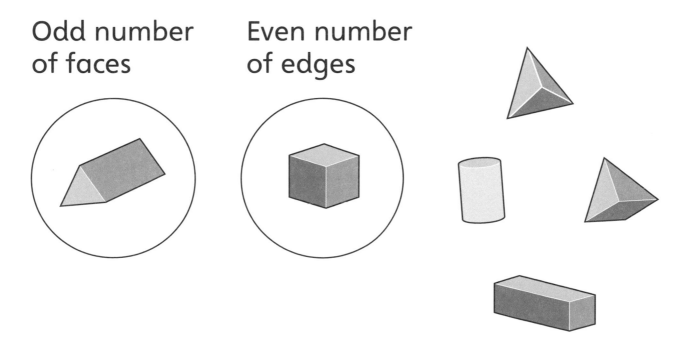

3 Tick the shape that could go in both groups.

Has a curved surface

Has no circular face

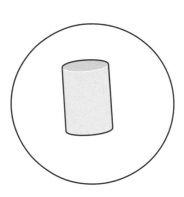

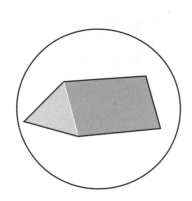

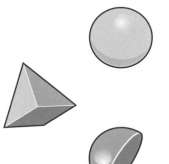

4 Choose headings to sort these shapes into two groups.

Make sure no shape is left out.

_____

_____

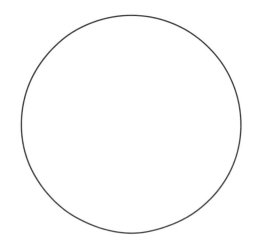

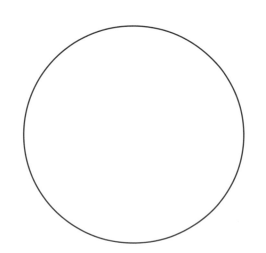

⑤

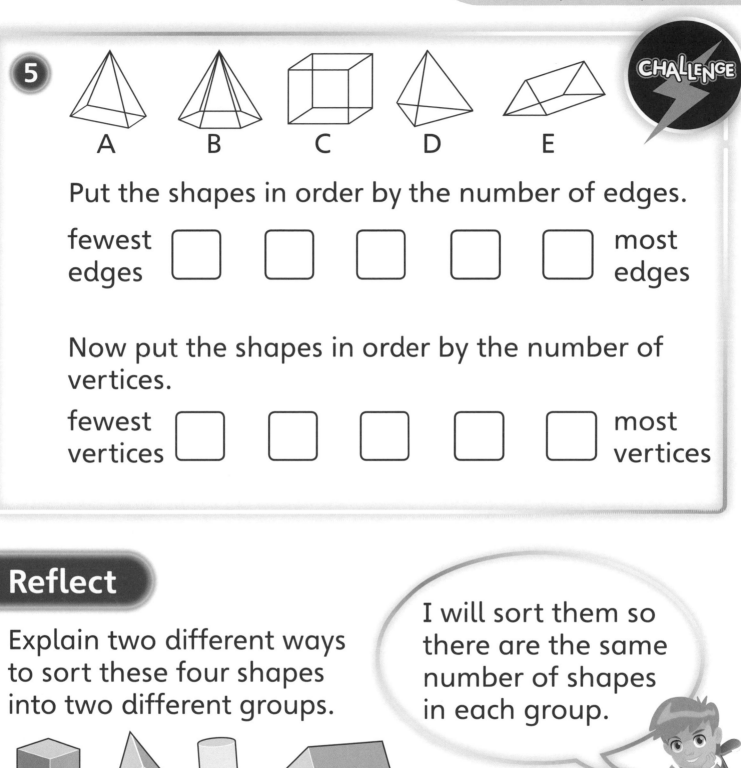

CHALLENGE

A   B   C   D   E

Put the shapes in order by the number of edges.

fewest
edges   ☐ ☐ ☐ ☐ ☐   most
edges

Now put the shapes in order by the number of vertices.

fewest
vertices   ☐ ☐ ☐ ☐ ☐   most
vertices

Reflect

Explain two different ways to sort these four shapes into two different groups.

I will sort them so there are the same number of shapes in each group.

1 _____

2 _____

→ Textbook 2B p148

Making patterns with 3D shapes

1 Write the names of the missing shapes.

a)
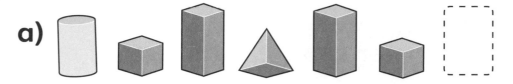

_____

b)
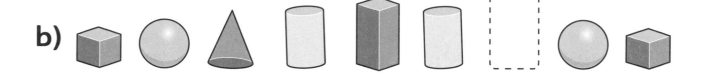

_____

c)
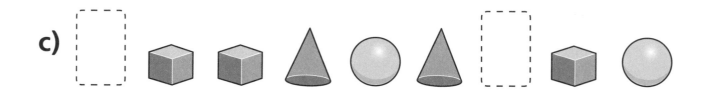

_____   _____

2 Number the boxes to show how to make a symmetrical pattern using each set of shapes.

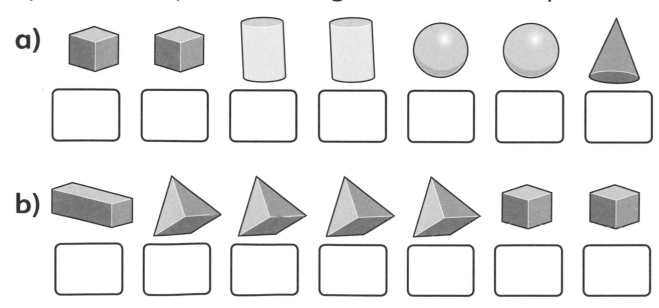

3 Make two different symmetrical patterns with these shapes.

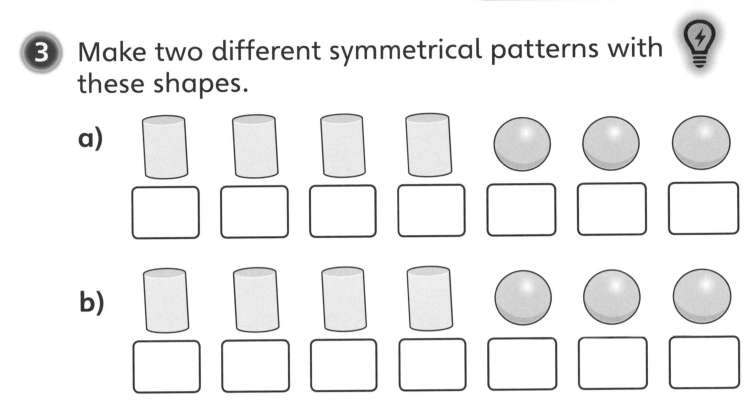

a)

b)

4 Create your own symmetrical pattern.

Hide two of the shapes.

Challenge your partner to guess the missing shapes.

Take it in turns.

Keep a tally of how many correct answers you each get.

Player A	
Player B	

5 **a)** Nate made a symmetrical pattern using three shapes.

CHALLENGE

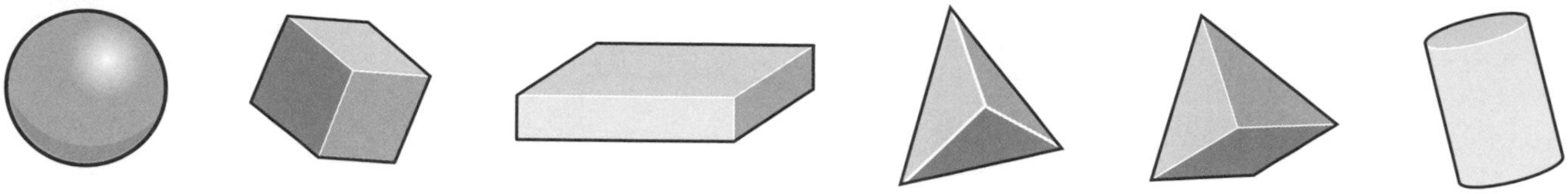

There were 16 faces in total.

Can you work out the shapes?

_____

_____

_____

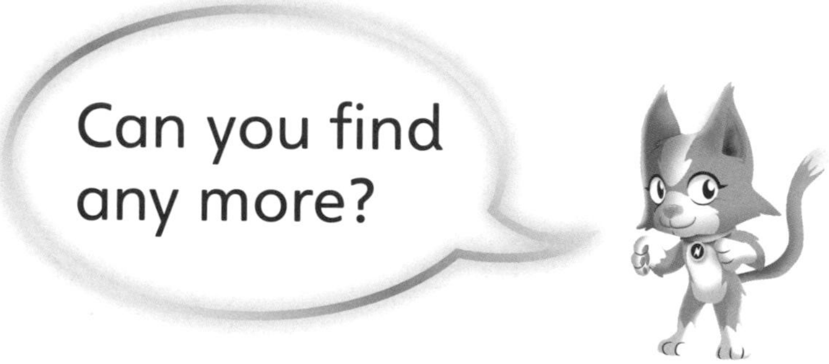

Can you find any more?

b) How many edges does Nate's pattern have?

_____

Reflect

Explain the difference between a symmetrical and a repeating pattern.

End of unit check

My journal

Theo has a square. He draws two straight lines on it and then cuts along them.

Now he has three new shapes.

He counts the number of vertices for each new shape.

Two of the shapes have three vertices.

One of the shapes has four vertices.

Find a way to cut the square into three shapes so each shape has a different number of vertices.

Is there more than one way?

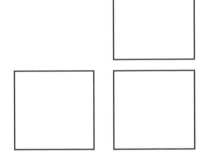

Describe your shapes to your partner.

I made two cuts so _____

_____ .

These words might help you.

vertices   **sides**

pentagon   **hexagon**

triangle

Power check

How do you feel about your work in this unit?

Power puzzle

Take 24 cubes.

How many different cuboids can you make by joining them together?

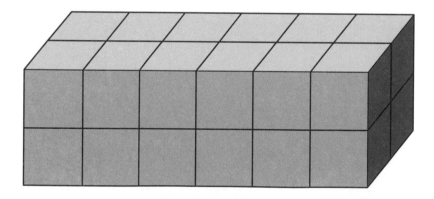

Take 27 cubes.

How many different cuboids can you make with them?

Introducing whole and parts

1 Match the part to the whole.

2 Complete the sentences about the truck.

Use some of the words in the list.

wheel	truck
light	bumper
window	

The _____ is the whole.

The _____ is a part.

The _____ is the whole.

The _____ is a part.

3 Write two sentences about these images.

a) The _____ is the whole and the

_____ is a part.

b) The flour is a _____ and the cake is the

_____ .

4 For each image, write two sentences about the whole and parts:

CHALLENGE

a) _____

_____

b)  _____

_____

5 A window is the part.

What could the whole be?

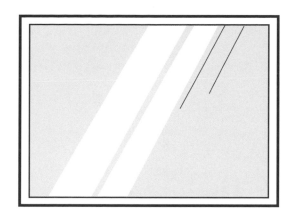

Can you think of three answers?

_____

_____

_____

Reflect

Choose an item in the classroom.

Make up sentences using part and whole.

_____

_____

_____

_____

_____

115

→ Textbook 2B p160

Making equal parts

1 Complete the sentences.

a)

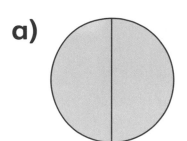

There are ☐ equal parts.

b)

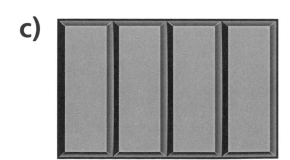

There are ☐ equal parts.

c)

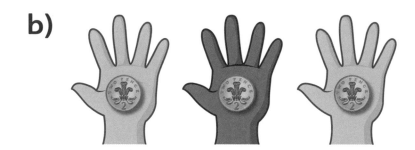

There are ☐ equal parts.

2 Complete each sentence using equal or unequal.

a)

The  is split into _____ parts.

b)

The is split into _____ parts.

c)

The  is split into _____ parts.

3 Draw lines to sort the shapes.

Equal parts		Unequal parts

117

4 Make the groups equal.

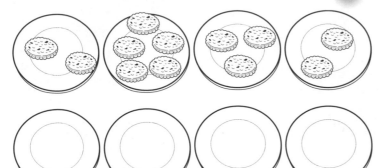

I can use cubes to represent the biscuits.

5 Get two pieces of paper.
Fold one into equal parts.
Fold one into unequal parts.

CHALLENGE

I wonder how many ways I can make 2 equal parts.

Reflect

There are 2 equal parts.

Do you agree?
Explain your answer.

Recognising a half ($\frac{1}{2}$)

1 Tick which of these show $\frac{1}{2}$ shaded.

a)
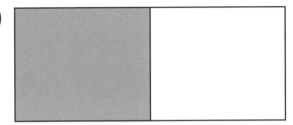

c)
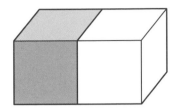

b)
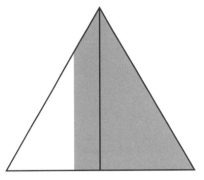

d)
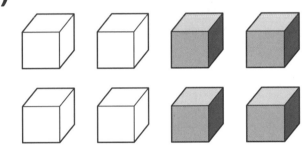

2 Shade $\frac{1}{2}$ of each shape.

a)

c)
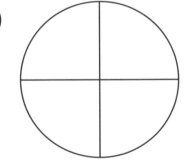

b)

d)

119

3 Here is $\frac{1}{2}$ of the shape.

Draw the whole.

a)

c)

b)

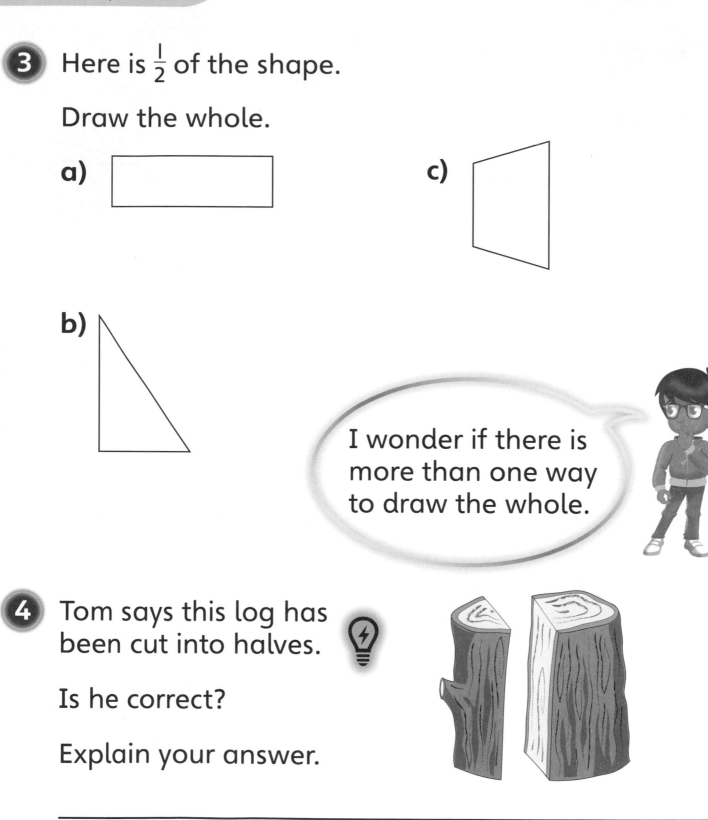

I wonder if there is more than one way to draw the whole.

4 Tom says this log has been cut into halves.

Is he correct?

Explain your answer.

_____

_____

_____

5 Which diagrams show $\frac{1}{2}$ shaded?

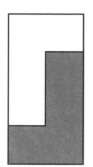 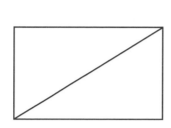 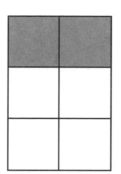

Explain one of your answers.

_____

_____

Reflect

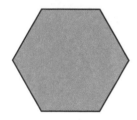  

Tick the shapes that can be split into two equal parts. Explain your answer.

 _____

 _____

 _____

_____

→ Textbook 2B p168

Finding a half

1 **a)** Complete the number sentences.

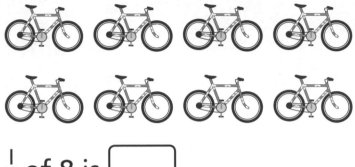

$\frac{1}{2}$ of 8 is ⬜.

b)

$\frac{1}{2}$ of 12 is ⬜.

2 Shade $\frac{1}{2}$ of each shape.

Complete the number sentence.

a)

$\frac{1}{2}$ of 10 is ⬜.

b)

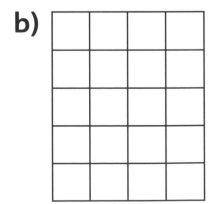

$\frac{1}{2}$ of 20 is ⬜.

3 Circle one half of each amount.

Complete the number sentence.

a)

$\frac{\boxed{}}{\boxed{}}$ of 24 is $\boxed{}$.

b)

$\frac{\boxed{}}{\boxed{}}$ of 18 is $\boxed{}$.

4 Work out each fraction and match it to the answer.

$\frac{1}{2}$ of 28   15

$\frac{1}{2}$ of 22   13

$\frac{1}{2}$ of 30   14

$\frac{1}{2}$ of 26   11

5 Tom and Mo share these sweets.

Can they share them equally? Explain your answer.

_____

_____

6 **a)** Cassie has some marbles.

Here are half of them.

The rest are in the jar.

How many marbles does Cassie have in total?

Cassie has [ ] marbles in total.

b) $\frac{1}{2}$ of [ ] = 7

Reflect

I can find $\frac{1}{2}$ of 16 by

_____

_____

Recognising a quarter ($\frac{1}{4}$)

1 Draw a line to show where each shape should go.

Shows $\frac{1}{4}$		Does not show $\frac{1}{4}$

2 Shade $\frac{1}{4}$ of each shape.

 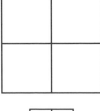 

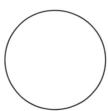 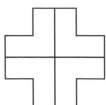 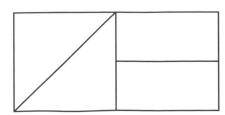

3 Here is $\frac{1}{4}$ of the shape.

Draw the full shape.

a)

b)

4 Is Joe correct?

Explain how you know.

I have split this stick of rock to show $\frac{1}{4}$.

5 How many different ways can you shade in $\frac{1}{4}$?

Draw more squares if you need to.

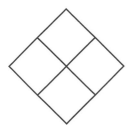 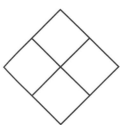 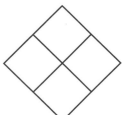 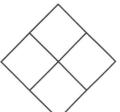

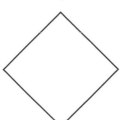 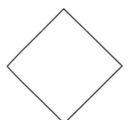 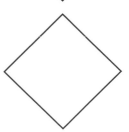 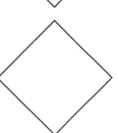

Reflect

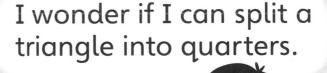

Tick the shapes that can be split into quarters.

Explain your answer.

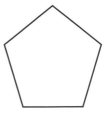

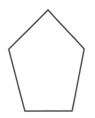 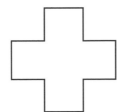 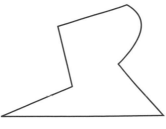 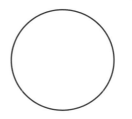

I ticked the shapes that _____

_____

_____

Finding a quarter

1 Share the counters equally into four groups.

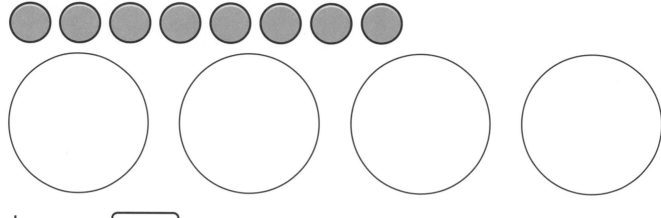

$\frac{1}{4}$ of 8 = ☐

2 Sita has **20** flowers.

She shares them between four vases equally.

How many flowers are in each vase?

I can draw the flowers in the vases.

$\frac{1}{4}$ of ☐ = ☐

There are ☐ flowers in each vase.

3 **a)** Shade $\frac{1}{4}$ of the shape.　　**b)** What is $\frac{1}{4}$ of 40?

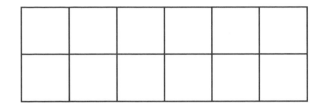

$\frac{1}{4}$ of ⬚ = ⬚　　　　$\frac{1}{4}$ of 40 = ⬚

4 Kiki shares some sweets between four bags.

Complete the number sentence.

$\frac{⬚}{⬚}$ of ⬚ is ⬚.

5 Half of a number is 6.

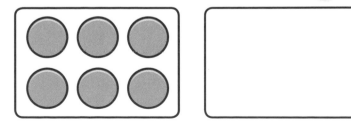

What is $\frac{1}{4}$ of the number?

$\frac{1}{4}$ of the number is ⬚.

6

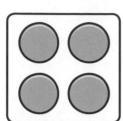    

One quarter is 4.

What is the whole?

$\frac{1}{4}$ of [ ] = 4

The whole is [ ].

Reflect

Choose fewer than 30 counters.

Can you share your counters in four equal groups?

Try with different numbers of counters.

Write number sentences when you make four equal groups.

$\frac{1}{4}$ of [ ] = [ ]

_____

_____

Unit fractions

1 Complete the sentences for each shape.

a) There are ☐ equal parts.

There is ☐ part shaded.

☐/☐ is shaded.

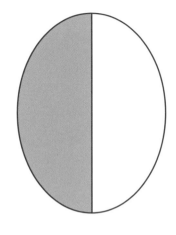

b) There are ☐ equal parts.

There is ☐ part shaded.

☐/☐ is shaded.

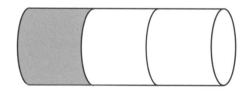

2 Tick the shapes that show $\frac{1}{3}$ shaded.

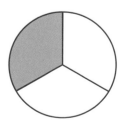 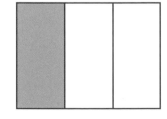 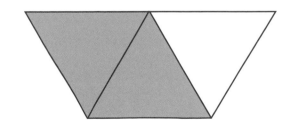 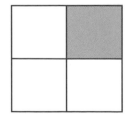

3 Circle the shapes that show a unit fraction shaded.

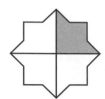    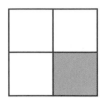 

4 Shade $\frac{1}{3}$ of this shape.

5 Draw the rest of each shape from the unit fraction.

a)

$\frac{1}{4}$

b)

$\frac{1}{3}$

6 What is $\frac{1}{3}$ of 12?

$\frac{1}{3}$ of 12 = ☐

7 There are 12 sweets.

Match each unit fraction to the number of sweets.

CHALLENGE

Unit fraction	Sweets
$\frac{1}{2}$	3
$\frac{1}{3}$	6
$\frac{1}{4}$	4

Reflect

Draw a flag where the fraction shaded yellow is a unit fraction.

I know that the fraction shaded yellow is a unit

fraction because _____

_____ .

→ Textbook 2B p184

Understanding other fractions

1 Complete the sentences.

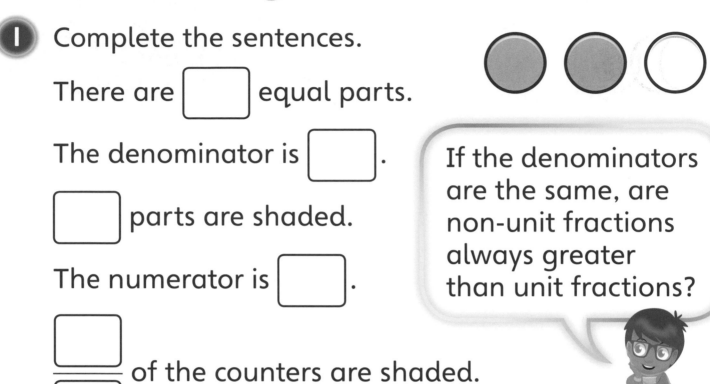

There are ☐ equal parts.

The denominator is ☐.

☐ parts are shaded.

The numerator is ☐.

$\dfrac{☐}{☐}$ of the counters are shaded.

If the denominators are the same, are non-unit fractions always greater than unit fractions?

2 Match each shape to the fraction shaded.

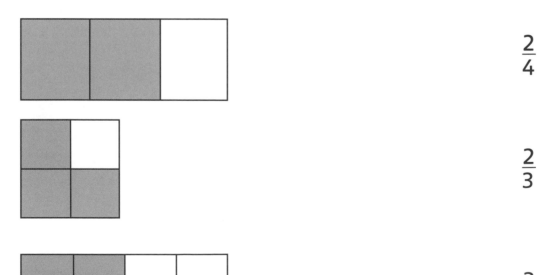

$\dfrac{2}{4}$

$\dfrac{2}{3}$

$\dfrac{3}{4}$

3 **a)** Shade $\frac{2}{3}$ of the balloons.

b) Circle $\frac{2}{4}$ of the bottles.

4 **a)** Do you agree with Sam?

I see $\frac{1}{3}$.

Explain your answer.

_____

_____

b) What fractions can you see?

Explain how you know.

☐ because _____

☐ because _____

135

5 Complete the fractions.

Non-unit fraction   Unit fraction

a)

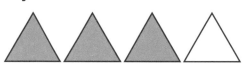

b)

Reflect

Circle all the non-unit fractions.

$\frac{2}{3}$ $\frac{1}{4}$ $\frac{3}{3}$ $\frac{1}{2}$ $\frac{1}{3}$ $\frac{2}{4}$ $\frac{3}{4}$

Draw one of them.

My drawing is a non-unit fraction because

$\frac{1}{2}$ and $\frac{2}{4}$

1 Tick the images that have $\frac{1}{2}$ shaded.

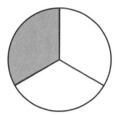 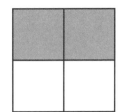 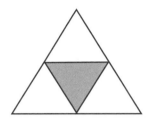 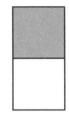

2 Shade $\frac{2}{4}$.

Shade $\frac{1}{2}$.

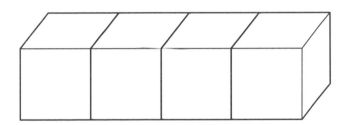 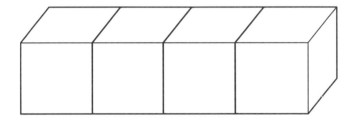

What do you notice?

_____

_____

I wonder if this is always the case.

3 Write in the missing fractions.

Match each statement to the fraction.

Less than $\frac{1}{2}$ Equal to $\frac{1}{2}$ Greater than $\frac{1}{2}$

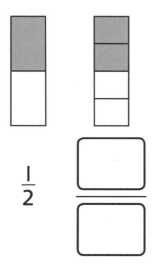

$\frac{1}{2}$

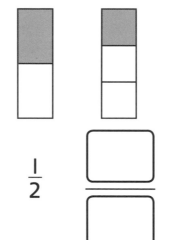

$\frac{1}{2}$

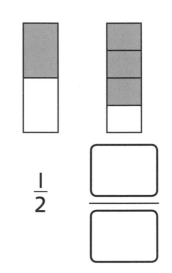

$\frac{1}{2}$

I can use the image of the $\frac{1}{2}$ to help.

4 Harry has $\frac{2}{4}$ of the cherries.

Ali has $\frac{1}{2}$ of the cherries.

They each have ☐ cherries.

They have the same amount

because $\frac{1}{2}$ and $\frac{2}{4}$ are _____ .

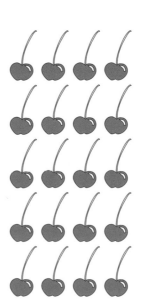

5 8 can be split into halves and quarters.

CHALLENGE

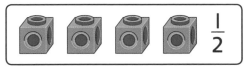

What other amounts can be split into halves **and** quarters?

Amounts that can be split into halves and quarters	Amounts that cannot be split into halves and quarters
8	

Reflect

Use a piece of paper or cubes to show that $\frac{1}{2}$ is equal to $\frac{2}{4}$.

- I used _____
- I showed that $\frac{1}{2}$ is equal to $\frac{2}{4}$ by _____
- _____
- _____
- _____

→ Textbook 2B p192

Finding $\frac{3}{4}$

1 Shade $\frac{3}{4}$ of each shape.

a)
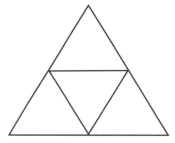

b)
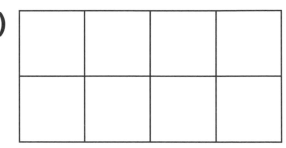

2 Tom has 12 sweets.

He shares them into four equal groups.

a) What is $\frac{1}{4}$ of Tom's sweets?

$\frac{1}{4}$ of 12 = ☐

b) What is $\frac{3}{4}$ of Tom's sweets?

$\frac{3}{4}$ of 12 = ☐

140

3 **a)** Jack has 16  and four pots.

He puts the same number of  into each pot.

How many  are in three pots?

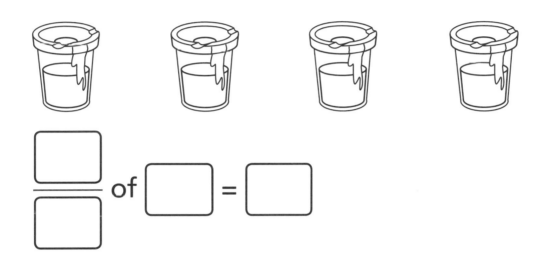

$\dfrac{\square}{\square}$ of $\square$ = $\square$

Jack puts $\square$  in each pot.

b) What is $\frac{1}{4}$ of 16?

$\frac{1}{4}$ of 16 = $\square$

4 What is $\frac{3}{4}$ of 20?

$\frac{3}{4}$ of 20 = $\square$

5 $\frac{3}{4}$ is 9.

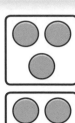

a) What is $\frac{1}{4}$?

$\frac{1}{4}$ is ☐.

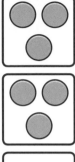

b) What is the whole?

The whole is ☐.

CHALLENGE

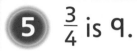

Reflect

$\dfrac{1}{4}$ $\dfrac{3}{4}$

unit fraction   non-unit fraction
numerator   denominator   quarters

What is the same about the fractions?

_____

_____

What is different?

_____

_____

Use the word list to help you.

Understanding a whole

1 What fraction of each shape is shaded?

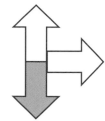 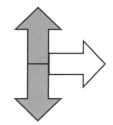 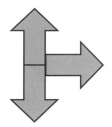

 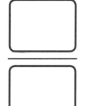 

2 Circle the fractions that show one whole.

   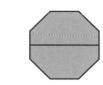

$\frac{1}{2}$ $\frac{2}{2}$ $\frac{3}{4}$ $\frac{4}{4}$

3 Match the fractions to make one whole.

4 Complete the number sentence to describe the picture.

a)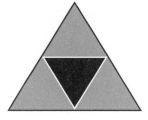

$$\frac{\square}{\square} + \frac{\square}{\square} = \frac{\square}{\square} = 1$$

b)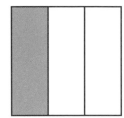

$$\frac{\square}{\square} + \frac{\square}{\square} = \frac{\square}{\square} = 1$$

5 Complete the number sentences.

a) $\frac{\square}{\square} + \frac{2}{3} = 1$

b) $\frac{3}{4} + \frac{\square}{\square} = 1$

c) $\frac{\square}{\square} + \frac{2}{4} = 1$

Can I complete this in more than one way?

CHALLENGE

6 Jemima ate 3 slices of cake.

Sam ate 2 slices of cake.

They both ate the same amount of cake.

Explain how this is possible.

_____

_____

_____

Reflect

When the numerator and the denominator are the same, the fraction equals one whole.

Circle if this statement is

   always true   sometimes true   never true

Write and draw fractions to prove your answer.

145

→ **Textbook 2B p200**

Understanding whole and parts

1 **a)** How many apples are there altogether?

There are $\boxed{}\dfrac{\boxed{}}{\boxed{}}$ apples.

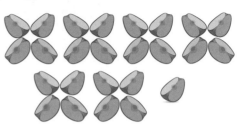

b) How many cakes are there altogether?

There are $\boxed{}\dfrac{\boxed{}}{\boxed{}}$ cakes.

2 Complete the .

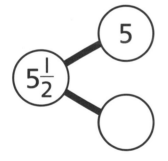
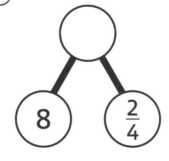
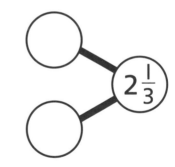

3 Circle the pictures that show $2\frac{1}{4}$.

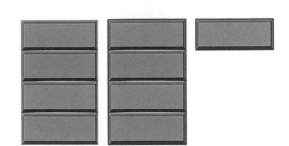

4

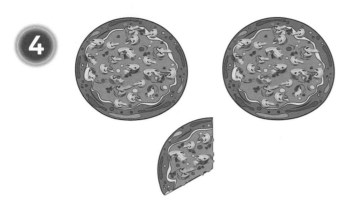

a) How many pizzas are there?

There are □ $\frac{\square}{\square}$ pizzas.

b) What fraction is needed to make 5 whole pizzas?

$\frac{\square}{\square}$ is needed to make 5 whole pizzas.

5 Tina and Raj share these oranges.

How many oranges do they each get?

Tina and Raj each get □ $\frac{\square}{\square}$ oranges.

6 Complete the in two ways.

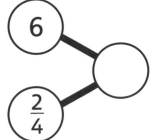   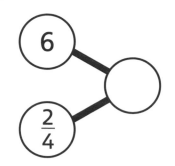

Reflect

Draw a picture using wholes and parts.

Ask your partner to write the fraction for your picture.

Describe what your picture shows.

Counting in halves

 Complete the sentences.

a)

This shows ☐ whole and ☐ half.

This is 1 $\dfrac{\Box}{\Box}$.

Circle what comes next if you are counting

in halves.   3   2 $2\frac{1}{2}$

 b)

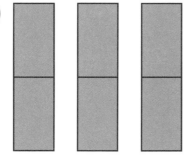

This shows ☐ wholes and ☐ halves.

This is ☐.

Circle what comes next if you are counting

in halves. $2\frac{1}{2}$ $3\frac{1}{2}$ 4

2 Adam is counting up in halves.

Fill in the missing numbers.

a) 0, $\frac{1}{2}$, 1, $1\frac{1}{2}$, 2, [ ] , [ ] , [ ]

b) 3, $3\frac{1}{2}$, [ ] , [ ] , [ ] , $5\frac{1}{2}$, 6

c)

8				10

3 Complete the table.

	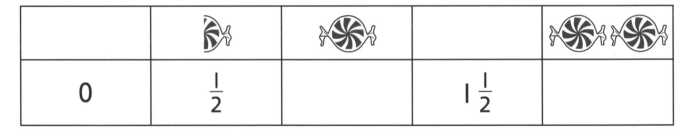			
0	$\frac{1}{2}$		$1\frac{1}{2}$	

4 Complete the number line.

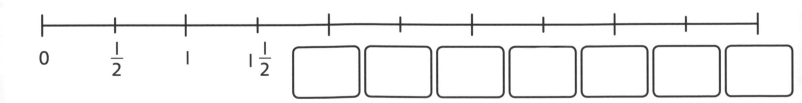

0    $\frac{1}{2}$ 1 $1\frac{1}{2}$ [ ] [ ] [ ] [ ] [ ] [ ] [ ]

5 **a)** Maya is counting in halves.

Explain her mistake.

$0, \frac{1}{2}, 1, 1\frac{1}{2}, 2, 3\frac{1}{2}$

_____

_____

b) Bob is counting in halves.

Explain his mistake.

$7, 6\frac{1}{2}, 6, 5, 4\frac{1}{2}, 4$

_____

_____

Reflect

$0, \frac{1}{2}, 1, 1\frac{1}{2}, 2$

I know the next number is ⬜ because

_____

→ **Textbook 2B p208**

Counting in quarters

1 Class 2A is making floor tiles.

Each tile is made of 4 parts:

How many whole tiles can be made from these parts?

[　　] whole tiles can be made.

2 Fill in the missing numbers.

a) $0, \frac{1}{4}, \frac{2}{4},$ [　　] , [　　] , [　　]

b)

$2\frac{3}{4}$	3	$3\frac{1}{4}$			4	

c)

2	$1\frac{3}{4}$	$1\frac{2}{4}$			

3 Fill in the numbers on the number lines.

a)

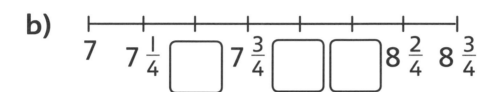

0 ☐ $\frac{2}{4}$ $\frac{3}{4}$ 1 $1\frac{1}{4}$ $1\frac{2}{4}$ ☐ 2 $2\frac{1}{4}$ $2\frac{2}{4}$ ☐

b)

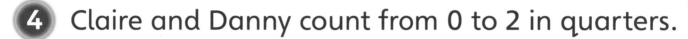

7 $7\frac{1}{4}$ ☐ $7\frac{3}{4}$ ☐ ☐ $8\frac{2}{4}$ $8\frac{3}{4}$

4 Claire and Danny count from 0 to 2 in quarters.

Claire: 0, $\frac{1}{4}$, $\frac{2}{4}$, $\frac{3}{4}$, 1, $1\frac{1}{4}$, $1\frac{2}{4}$, $1\frac{3}{4}$, 2.

Danny: 0, $\frac{1}{4}$, $\frac{1}{2}$, $\frac{3}{4}$, 1, $1\frac{1}{4}$, $1\frac{1}{2}$, $1\frac{3}{4}$, 2.

Who is correct?

Explain your answer.

I wonder if they can both be correct.

_____

_____

5 Jon has five chocolate bars.

He eats $\frac{1}{4}$ of a bar each day for 10 days.

How many chocolate bars does he have left?

Jon has ☐☐/☐ chocolate bars left.

Reflect

$0, \frac{1}{4}, \frac{2}{4}, \frac{3}{4}, 1, 1\frac{1}{4}$

I know the next number is ☐ because

_____

→ Textbook 2B p212

End of unit check

My journal

Here are eight fractions.

$\frac{1}{4}$ $\frac{1}{2}$ $\frac{1}{3}$ $\frac{2}{4}$ $\frac{3}{4}$ $\frac{2}{2}$ $\frac{4}{4}$ $\frac{3}{3}$

Sort the fractions into groups.

Explain how you have sorted them.

_____

_____

_____

These words might help you.

unit fraction

non-unit fraction

whole

quarters

halves

thirds

half

part

Power check

How do you feel about your work in this unit?

Power play

You will need:
- a dice
- a counter each

How to play:
- Take it in turns to roll the dice and move your counter.
- If you land on a picture, write it as a fraction.
- If you land on a fraction, draw it as a picture.
- If you get it wrong, move back to the start.
- The first person to reach the end wins.

$\frac{3}{3}$	$\frac{3}{4}$	▭	$\frac{2}{2}$	✚	$\frac{1}{3}$	◕	End
▦							
$\frac{1}{2}$							
◓	✳	$\frac{4}{4}$	◴	◔	$\frac{1}{4}$	▤	Start

My Power Points

Colour in the ☆ to show what you have learned.

Colour in the ☺ if you feel happy about what you have learned.

Unit 6

I can ...

☆ ☺ Share equally between groups

☆ ☺ Recognise odd and even numbers

☆ ☺ Use the 2 times-table to help me divide by 2

☆ ☺ Use the 5 times-table to help me divide by 5

☆ ☺ Use the 10 times-table to help me divide by 10

☆ ☺ Use a bar model to help me group and share

Unit 7

I can ...

☆ ☺ Make a tally chart

☆ ☺ Make a pictogram and explain what it shows

☆ ☺ Explain what a block diagram shows

Unit 8

I can …

☆ ☺ Measure lengths and heights in centimetres
☆ ☺ Measure lengths and heights in metres
☆ ☺ Compare and order lengths and heights

Unit 9

I can …

☆ ☺ Recognise 2D and 3D shapes
☆ ☺ Count the sides on 2D shapes
☆ ☺ Explain what vertex and vertices means
☆ ☺ Find lines of symmetry
☆ ☺ Count faces, edges and vertices on 3D shapes
☆ ☺ Make patterns with shapes

Unit 10

I can …

☆ ☺ Use the words **whole** and **parts** when talking about fractions
☆ ☺ Recognise $\frac{1}{2}$ and find a $\frac{1}{2}$ of a quantity
☆ ☺ Recognise $\frac{1}{4}$ and find a $\frac{1}{4}$ of a quantity
☆ ☺ Explain what a unit fraction is
☆ ☺ Explain what a non-unit fraction is
☆ ☺ Count in halves and quarters

Keep up the good work!

Notes

Notes